LOST FOR WORDS

THE PSYCHOANALYSIS OF ANOREXIA AND BULIMIA

EM FARRELL

OTHER

Other Press
New York

LOST FOR WORDS

Anorexics and bulimics are lost for words. Most are women. They feel they have no way to communicate effectively. They have not found the words to express and name the turmoil of their experience to themselves or others. This leaves them in a world where neither food nor words can provide nourishment and sustenance. This book explores the nature of anorexia and bulimia, paying particular attention to the issues of mortality and the complexities of the mother-daughter relationship. It stresses the importance for technique of understanding the violent and agonising nature of these individuals' inner worlds. The author has worked with over 180 women with eating disorders.

The history of theories and treatments of eating disorders is thoroughly canvassed, and the book provides the most comprehensive review of the psychoanalytic literature in print. It draws, in particular, on the Kleinian tradition and the work of Winnicott.

Em Farrell is a psychoanalytic psychotherapist in private practice. She lectures and is a tutor at Regent's College School of Psychotherapy and Counselling and has been a member of the Eating Disorders Workshop at the Tavistock Clinic.

10 9 8 7 6 5 4 3

Library of Congress Cataloging-in-Publication Data

Farrell, Em.
    Lost for words : the psychoanalysis of anorexia and bulimia / Em Farrell.
        p. cm.
    Originally published: London : Process Press, 1995.
    Includes bibliographical references and index.
    ISBN 1-892746-56-5 (sc : alk. paper)
    1. Anorexia nervosa. 2. Bulimia. 3. Psychoanalysis. I. Title.

RC552.A5 F37 2000
616.85'26—dc21

                                                                  00-027707

For Bob and Nanci

Contents

Acknowledgements

I would like to acknowledge the support and help of the following people: Robin and Louisa Lane Fox, Peter and Diana Balfour, Robin Piper, Karen Proner, Barbara Reid, and Christopher Fyfe who helped and supported me through my years of university education. I would like to thank Brett Kahr and David Smith for making this book a better one than it would otherwise have been – both through their teaching and their comments. Vivienne Lewin helped me to understand and to bear much of the turbulence encountered in my work. Thanks to Dido, Gerry and Jo for their support. To Bernard for his. Alison, Iwona and Corinne took me and continue to take me happily away from my books. Thanks to my parents whose lives are so removed from those in this book and to my patients for sharing theirs with me. Thanks to the Eating Disorder Workshop at the Tavistock, particularly to Arthur Hyatt and Gianna Williams, who provided much useful food for thought. My ideas began to crystallize after reading the work of Harvey Schwartz and David Krueger, to whom I shall always be indebted. Finally, thanks to Bob Young, for providing me with a structure, for pointing out the ideas that needed more thought, for reading the manuscript, more than once, for impatiently correcting my grammar, for publishing it and ...

Preface

Sub-clinical eating disorder, (SED), is a new and nasty fact of life (Hsu, 1990, p. 119; Lerner, 1993, pp. 110–13). It is estimated that up to 80 per cent of women suffer from it (Coward, 1993, p. 157), approximately the number who are concerned about their weight or dieting in the United Kingdom at any one time. SED does not threaten life, but it is a low-key, persistent form of eating disorder which limits women's lives and their potential. One strand of SED is yo-yo dieting, a term which describes people who go on and off diets over a period of years. The negative effect of yo-yo dieting is that an individual's metabolism slows down to such an extent that in order to remain at a normal weight she has to eat less. If she eats her normal diet, she would put on weight. It should have been the death knell of dieting as a way of life and caught the popular imagination in such books as Geoffrey Cannon's and Hetty Einseg's *Stop Dieting Because Dieting Makes You Fat* (1983) and Shelley Bovey's *Being Fat Is Not a Sin* (1989). It was not, despite the increasing evidence that diets made you fat, that 98 per cent of diets fail, with 90 per cent of individuals ending up weighing more when they stopped dieting altogether than they did before they began. These figures are commonly cited, for example in Susie Orbach's *Fat Is a Feminist Issue* (1979) and Kim Chernin's *Womansize* (1983). In *Bulimarexia* (1987) Marlene Boskind-White and William C. White say, 'Thus, dieting actually leads to an increase in the number of fat cells stored' (p. 160).

The figure of 80 per cent is an estimate, but it means that only 20 per cent of women are not obsessed with food in some way. SED is a disorder because it has been found that the effects of persistent and intermittent dieting produce similar symptoms in individuals as starvation itself does (Duker and Slade, 1988). This is a frightening thought. It means that an overwhelming majority of women are unwell as a direct result of their relationship to food. This is in addition to the emotional or psychological effects of being preoccupied with food, weight and body size. Women express shock, horror and outrage at severe anorexic and bulimic conditions. From my clinical experience of working with women, I think the shock is feigned, a defence erected in order to protect themselves from the realisation of the blurred boundaries between dieting, SED and full-blown eating disorders. Women can identify all too easily with starving and bingeing. What is harder to identify with is when having an eating disorder becomes a way of life, when the psychological and emotional preoccupation with food becomes all-encompassing at the expense of relationships, work and play.

The distinction is between the degree and the nature of the preoccupation with eating, food, weight and body image. Many women may feel terrorised by a pair of scales or the thought of a chocolate eclair, but few will weigh themselves up to 500 times a day, or eat 20 eclairs, before making themselves sick. These figures and the following descriptions are based on my clinical experience with patients. Some anorexics spend years of their lives counting calories; that is all they do, running totals of yesterday, the day before, last week, the binge that broke the lowest total of the week. Anorexics become skeletal in mind as well as body – nothing is to remain, just what is not to be eaten and how to survive the day, convincing those around you that everything is fine. Some bulimics spend all their day bingeing and vomiting; they do nothing else. They may walk the streets furtively, hoping their frequent visits to the same sweet shops and bakeries are not being noticed, and, if they imagine they are, going further afield in order to feed their habit.

These are extremes, but up to 18 per cent of anorexics die from their illness, and bulimics occasionally do (*Diagnostic and Statistical Manual III-R*, 1988, p. 66). Anorexics die from starvation either directly or indirectly. A bulimic can die from a burst oesophagus or as the result of a stomach rupture. Laxative abuse and vomiting can severely disturb the electrolyte balance, which in turn can cause brain damage. It is frightening working with these women. An anorexic may collapse at any time, either on her way to a session, during one, or in between. Anorexic bulimics often have the additional problem of self-damaging behaviour in the form of overdoses of laxatives, alcohol, drugs or other pills. Normal weight bulimics are the least frightening group with which to work. They rarely die as a result of their eating disorder, although they often suffer from severe depression, and may be suicidal, but their eating disorder itself is less likely to kill them. All bulimics may suffer from the non-reversible erosion of the enamel on the teeth due to the action of stomach acid in vomit and all groups risk the increased likelihood of developing osteoporosis.

One in five women is likely to suffer from an eating disorder, anorexia or bulimia, not SED, during their lifetime (Dally, 1989). Official figures suggest that there are nine female anorexics to each male anorexic (Crisp and Toms, 1972). Figures for the proportion of male to female bulimics are much more apocryphal, with its prevalence being cited among ballet dancers, models and jockeys. Eating disorders are not bound by age, length of time, intensity or specificity. Here are a few examples of women I have worked with or known: a woman of 35 who was bulimic for three weeks during a difficult time in her life, a woman of 60 who was anorexic for 30 years, a woman of 45 who was anorexic at 17, bulimic at 25 and a compulsive eater from 35 onwards. Eating disorders do not have a set course, a set outcome or a set meaning. People who have eating disorders are, however, united by a common feeling of alienation and deep internal distress. They try to assuage, modify, or bury this distress, either by eating or by *not* eating.

I have worked, first in a humanistic and then in an increasingly psychodynamic way with over 170 women with eating problems, mainly bulimics, both normal weight and anorexic. My interest has been held by the tremendous struggles these women go through, in order to find a way of relating to themselves, to others and to the world at large. I am going to focus on this problem of how these women relate in the chapters which follow.

I decided on the title, *Lost for Words*, for a number of reasons, all of which are connected to the recognition that words are as, if not more, problematic for women with eating disorders than their relationship to food. They are either seen as a useless form of communciation, or as being tremendously powerful, so powerful that they may drown in them, or be torn to pieces by them. The pre-verbal, concrete way these women often think and relate make words both a dangerous and unwanted commodity. Finding words, in contrast to being lost, frustrated or attacked by them, suggests a capacity for communication which recognises the presence of another and the possibility of successful projection and introjection. As one of my patients said, 'Words are useless, I want to *make* you feel what I feel, words are no good.' For her, the only satisfactory state of communication was two people feeling intensely and identically, in phantasy a state of fusion, of non-differentiation. Difference has implicitly to be acknowledged when words are used to attempt communication.

This point is well made by Dana Birksted-Breen in her paper 'Working with an Anorexic Patient' where her patient was so reluctant to talk that she says 'I sometimes had the fantasy that she and I were buried in a tomb of silence for eternity' (1989, p. 32). The problem for both anorexics and bulimics is how to make a gainful and durable link – an internal link to an object that can in some way be allowed to be good. This is an essential precursor and integral part of the working through of the Oedipal situation.

I do not want to claim more or less for this study than is appropriate. What I hope to do by looking at the pre-Freudian, Freudian and post-Freudian approaches is to demonstrate why many eating disordered patients live in almost permanently endangered internal territory. One of the frequent questions that occurs when working with these patients is whether their internal experience can be amelio-rated by therapy. There is an implicit tendency in the psychoanalytic literature and in clinical practice towards hopelessness and helplessness when working with anorexics and bulimics. One of my aims is to focus on this despair and, by exploring the different individual psychoanalytic under-standings of eating disorders, to try to understand it. To do this I shall use Winnicott's ideas of transitional objects and transitional space to explore the mother–daughter relationship, the bulimic symptom and the transference and countertransference. The first two topics are considered in Chapter Three and the last in Chapter Four. By so doing I hope to indicate ways of understanding which can perhaps provide the opportunity of a different and more benign and nourishing link being very gradually established within the therapy and the internal worlds of these patients.

My usual theoretical and clinical approach is more clearly Kleinian. This means that in this book I have not had the space to do sufficient justice to pathological narcissism, pathological organisations, envy, two-and-three dimensionality and problems of thinking . I shall also leave the field of cultural, social and feminist theory and understanding to others and concentrate on what I have learnt from my direct experience of working individually with these patients. When in the course of this book I offer generalisations about patients with eating disorders without citing references, these conclusions are offered as inductions from my own clinical experience.

When I had completed the first draft of this book, a friend directed me to Joyce McDougall's *Theatres of the Body* (1989), where I found similar, although not identical, ideas to my own. This coincidence provided a welcome confirmation of the validity of my insights, although I wished I had read her books before I had started on my own. She covers similar ground in linking a mother's narcissistic preoccupation with her child, and her difficulties in allowing her to separate, to a later disturbance in the function and development of transitional objects. It is in the area of what constitutes a transitional object, even nascently, that I think my views differ from hers. She would, I think, view bingeing (both the eating and the food) as being pathological transitional objects. My own understanding is that this behaviour represents an attempt to find, mimic, recreate an experience of an internal mother, a stage before the use of any kind of a transitional object is possible. What happens next is where I would look for a transitional object of some kind, an area where rest or play may be experienced.

CHAPTER 1

Introduction

Eating is normal, in that it is a human necessity; having an eating disorder is not. Sours (1980, p. 205) suggests that a form of anorexia was recognised as early as the eleventh century. The meaning attached to various religious practices involving self starvation is obviously contingent upon their historical, social, cultural and personal context. Over time, it is not possible to verify a homogeneity of symptoms and meanings. It is still worth asking questions. Did the Roman's occasional use of vomitorium ever lead to the development of bulimia, as current mass binges and collective vomiting among college students do in a minority of cases (Hogan, 1992). Is it possible to look through our 1990s eyes at the 'Holy women' of the thirteenth and fourteenth centuries and try to equate their behaviour with the disease we term anorexia nervosa? There is no current consensus on what the eating disorders are or indeed if they are a valid clinical category at all. There is no consensus on how they are understood or how they should be treated. It is a complicated and confusing matter.

What is certain is that despite the lack of clarity, the numbers of women and men suffering from some type of eating problem continues to increase. This is suggested by the numbers of articles written about bulimia in the last 16 years. In the years from 1977 to 1986 there were approximately 600 articles written on the topic of bulimia. In the last six years, from 1987 to 1993, around 1,500 articles have been published in learned journals. A parallel development can be seen in the media coverage of eating disorders. Media definitions of eating disorders have undergone dramatic shifts of emphasis in the last ten years or so. Stories have to be newsworthy, so it was the extreme cases that were reported in the early days, anorexics and bulimics who died of their illnesses. The media presented these individuals' behaviours as alien to their readers. Lists of what they ate, either very short or very long, were produced, and explanations of the disorders were given in strictly behavioural terms. They were both described as 'Slimmers Diseases'. Diets that went wrong made some people want to binge. For others, diets that went right prevented them from being able to eat very much at all. The impression was sensationalist, that anorexics and bulimics had no control over what they ate and that their behaviour was outrageous, yet fascinating. They were described as individuals indulging in overt rituals of greed, on the one hand, and denial of need, on the other.

A variety of psychological myths grew up, that anorexia was about not wanting to grow up, whereas bulimia was about wanting to have your cake and eat it, but without putting on weight. There is a strong element of truth in both of these statements and the self-outing of stars such as Jane Fonda, Margaux Hemingway and Bonnie Langford encouraged a more understanding and in-depth portrayal of these disorders. This culminated in the widespread reporting of a speech given by Princess Diana at the 1993 Eating Disorders Conference in London.

Obesity is rarely a matter for media interest – humour and pornography apart – but anorexia and bulimia are. Women's use and abuse of their bodies is infinitely interesting, and the extreme behaviour of some bulimics and anorexics has meant the picture presented by the media has remained split into two disorders, anorexia and bulimia. Cases of anorexia were reported in the media before cases of bulimia, and the number of books and articles on anorexia still outnumber those on bulimia. Bulimia is thought to be a relation of anorexia, perhaps a close one, but there is an imagined line between the two which has to be looked at if either or both of these disorders is to be understood.

To locate current understandings of eating disorders it is ideally desirable to try to disentangle the myriad ways of con-ceptualising and treating these disorders that have grown up over time. The philosophical split into mind and body is present from the seventeenth century onwards, and one way of negotiating a route through the mass of material is to look at approaches that saw anorexia nervosa as a primarily physical disorder as distinct from those that saw it as primarily an emotional or mental disorder. The latter leads to the exploration of the conscious and unconscious meanings of the symptoms, the former to drug and behavioural models of treatment. In the United States and the United Kingdom there is an increasing tendency for hospital regimes to combine approaches so that there is a psychodynamic component in treatment programmes, whether individual, family or group.

The emergence of a plethora of understandings of bulimia and anorexia means there will not be the room to survey in depth the many different approaches, both physical and emotional. Family therapy has been used to good result, particularly with young anorexics, who have not had the illness for more than three years. Minuchin (1974) and Palazzoli (1978) have successfully pioneered two different family therapy models for working with these patients. Christopher Fairburn's (1981, 1982) cognitive-behavioural approach to working with bulimics has also been successful, well documented and influential. The use of drug therapy is a much more contentious issue, as are hospitalisation and force feeding (Wilson et al., 1992). All of these approaches are dealing with the behaviour of the individual, as a member of a family system, or in relation to food. What is not being addressed is the meaning being given to the symptom itself, or to the individual's experience of life. My own approach is psychoanalytic. I have no doubt as to the efficacy, in terms of symptom reduction or cessation, of the approaches mentioned above. They do however focus on the symptom itself, whether from a personal or familial point of view. My interest lies in understanding the symptom in the context of these patients' internal and external worlds. I think more than the symptom has to change; it is not just about wanting to get a person to eat, or to stop bingeing, but to understand what it means for them in the intricate and complex interactions of their internal world.

I wish to look at individual *psychoanalytic* approaches to working with eating disordered patients as they have emerged over time. I shall look at pre-Freudian, Freudian and post-Freudian ways of understanding anorexia and bulimia. This approach has been elaborated and worked with by many ego psychologists in the United States. Simultaneously some of them have moved from an understanding of the Oedipal origin of these disorders (Greenacre, 1950, 1952; Fraiberg, 1972; Brenner, 1974; Hogan, 1985; Sperling, 1983) to an understanding of their pre-Oedipal origins (Jessner and Abse, 1960; Boris, 1984a, 1984b; Sperling, 1949, 1968; Sours, 1974; Palazzoli, 1978; Sprince, 1984; and Wilson, 1992a) and often (as Sperling's presence in both lists suggests) an appreciation of understanding different meanings within the same symptom complex. A Kleinian understanding of narcissistic disorders allows the two strands to coexist in a different way and has important implications for technique. The expression of surprisingly consistent technical difficulties which seem inherent in working with this group of patients led me to wonder about the nature of the connection between technique and theory, for example, the technical implications of adopting a deficit model of working with these patients, which tends to be more active and supportive than a classically analytic one.

The importance of the absence of transitional space and transitional phenomena is noted directly in some clinical papers (Sprince, 1984, 1988) and indirectly in others (Boris 1984a, 1984b, 1988; Rizzuto, 1988, Birksted-Breen 1989). However, there is little that is theoretical that has been written about eating disorders and transitional phenomena. An exception to this is a paper by Alan Sugarman and Cheryl Kurash on 'The Body as a Transitional Object in Bulimia' (1982). In the United Kingdom there is little psychoanalytic literature on working with adults with eating disorders. The papers which are written are usually good and based on individual work with one or two patients (Sohn, 1985; Coles, 1988; Sprince 1988, Birksted-Breen, 1989; Maguire, 1989). I wish to add a new angle which does not invalidate other perspectives, but which I hope offers an additional lens through which to perceive a particular aspect of the behaviour of some bulimics. I wish to explore in detail the idea of the body as a transitional object, but in a very different way from

Sugarman and Kurash. I shall also explore other aspects of bulimic rituals as ways and means of creating, finding or refinding some kind of a transitional experience.

At the same time, I shall try to explore and elucidate the differences and similarities between restrictor anorexics, bulimic anorexics and normal weight bulimics. This sounds a simple task but it is not. Even within the revised third edition of the *Diagnostic and Statistical Manual* (*DSM III-R*) of the American Psychiatric Association (1988) there are glaring ambiguities, and many psychotherapists working with anorexics and bulimics fail to define clearly the group to which they are referring. It does matter. What I shall show is that the symptom of the eating behaviour, whether eating too little, too much or alternating between the two, unifies understanding, but what splits it is the issue of weight – weight in the sense of closeness to death, whether consciously or unconsciously. This is what differentiates a number of normal weight bulimics from anorexics and anorexic bulimics. This may explain why, although the range of psychopathology can be very varied, there are striking similarities in the experience in the transference and countertransference relationship, as well as clear differences between these groups.

According to an object relations model as understood by Melanie Klein and her followers, knowing something of the different internal worlds of these patients is a prerequisite to understanding the nature of their eating disorders. Before moving into the sphere of the conscious and the unconscious phantasy life of bulimics and anorexics, I shall describe the current diagnostic categories in *DSM-III-R* to provide a framework of understanding and reference in which to move. To untangle the confusions by which the current categorisations are troubled, I shall give a brief overview of the historical emergence of these disorders and the relationships between them. I shall follow the two strands of the body and the mind, and, where appropriate, the conscious and unconscious understanding of the behaviour up to the present day.

Having surveyed the existing literature, the primitive and powerful nature of the experience of disturbed eating will, I hope, also explain the interest in the particular problems of technique that come to the fore when treating these patients. I hope to provide a study of how particular theories affect technique, and how others do not. I will also consider how some of the experiences in the transference and countertransference work with these patients has not been delved into sufficiently. I hope to illustrate the common elements which are present and need attention and understanding in working with these individuals. Depending on the psychoanalytic approach of the individual, different ways of working may need to be thought about at different times in the treatment – how to give interpretations and how they are likely to be understood. I shall consider this in the chapter on technique.

Definitions

Anorexia nervosa was included in the *Diagnostic and Statistical Manual of Mental Disorders DSM-I* 1952 as a psychophysiological reaction. In *DSM-II* (1968) it was under special symptoms – feeding disturbances. It was not until 1980 that bulimia was given an entry in the *DSM*. It joined anorexia, pica and rumination in the newly designated eating disorders section. Prior to this bulimia did not exist as a diagnostic category in its own right. Bulimic symptoms were listed as an occasional accompaniment to anorexia and psychogenic vomiting was a symptom often connected to other neurotic complexes and to psychotic ones (Parry Jones and Parry Jones, 1991). As early as Robert Whytt (1767) – whose detailed description of an anorexic boy included bingeing – the presence of bingeing, vomiting, diuretic and laxative taking has been visible at times among certain anorexics, Ellen West being one example (Binswanger, 1944). The creation of a separate bulimic category in *DSM-III* (1980) raises questions, both current and historical, about the nature of anorexia, of bulimia and the relationship between the two.

By stating that anorexics can suffer from bulimia, although bulimics cannot suffer from anorexia, the separating factor becomes that of weight. To be classified as anorexic, patients have to be 15 per cent below their normal weight. Bulimics do not. It is a defining symptom of anorexia and not of bulimia. Bulimia was recognised when it became apparent that individuals who had not had severe weight problems, who had been neither obese nor anorexic, were exhibiting bulimic symptoms. Little research has been done on this group, and the question of whether bulimia, as defined in *DSM-III-R*, represents a studiable and distinguishable group is still in dispute. Indeed writers and clinicians such as Sperling (1978), Stangler and Prinz (1980), Wilson (1983), Bruch (1985) and Wilson *et al.* (1992), refuse to recognise it is as being a separate syndrome from anorexia. They see bulimia as being part of the anorexic syndrome and so disown, by implication, the existence of normal weight bulimics. Anorexic bulimics are interestingly thought by Wilson to be the hardest group to treat, which implicitly puts his position into doubt. He describes them as 'the most difficult and refractory anorexic patients' (Wilson, 1983, p. 170).

Before moving on to the specifics of *DSM-III-R*, I would like to describe a bulimic, an anorexic and an anorexic bulimic, as they might present in the consulting room. I am describing an extreme example of each sufferer. These descriptions are based on patients whom I have seen, and whose visual state is very striking. The symptoms described can be found in most self-help books about eating disorders, for example Marilyn Duker and Roger Slade's *Anorexia Nervosa and Bulimia: How To Help* (1988). An anorexic is instantly spottable. She is usually extremely thin. She is starving. Her eyes are often sunken, her face cadaverous. Her facial bones look as though they are trying to break through her stretched and fragile-looking skin. Her hands may be red and swollen and look too large for her body. Her gums may be receding and there may be a layer of baby-like hair, lanugo, over her face and body. The thinness of her body, of bones lacking adequate lubrication and supporting muscles, makes one wonder whether movement itself is possible. Where can her energy come from and how can the pain be tolerated? Yet she might present herself as being well, as though this state of extreme thinness is not connected to her as a person at all, or if it is, it is a desired, not an unwanted state.

In my experience anorexic bulimics sometimes look a little healthier. This is often an illusion, a result of the swelling of the salivary glands which make the face, cheeks and neck bulge. This is a response to the body's attempt to take nourishment from the moment food enters the mouth. The food does not remain in the body for long, and the salivary glands become more than usually sensitive to food in the mouth and attempt to get the maximum nourishment they can from this first site of digestion. A bulimic anorexic has a definite presence. There is a sense of having a person in the room, often a very angry, smelly, distrustful person, but a person. The feeling of being non-existent, of the absence, or severe retreat – of the withdrawal of the self which is so pronounced an experience with anorexics – is not there with anorexic bulimics, whose unwanted, out of control, unheeded and messy self is forcefully present in the room.

A normal weight bulimic is unnoticeable by physical appearance alone. Some are dressed in a careful and feminine fashion, some in a more male and chaotic manner. Some are smart, some are scruffy. Many are good looking. Some look you in the eye, some do not. There is little to let you know they are bulimic unless they come to the session in the middle of a binge, in which case the feeling of being in a maelstrom is unavoidable. But physically, little is apparent. What might be visible are tiny broken veins on the cheeks and, depending on the severity of the disorder, the presence of calluses (Russell, 1979), grazes, or red marks on the hands, particularly the knuckles and sometimes the fingers. This is due to the action of the teeth against the hand when it is thrust into the mouth to induce vomiting. A normal weight bulimic may have swollen salivary glands, but in an average or above average weight individual this is not necessarily noticeable.

So differences are definitely apparent from the outside in, suggesting, according to a modern Kleinian approach, a difference in the underlying phantasies between the two (Klein, 1920, 1923; Isaacs, 1948). In *DSM-III-R* pica and rumination are seen as disconnected childhood disorders, while anorexia and bulimia are seen as connected eating disorders which occur during adolescence and early adulthood. Pica, the consumption of non-food items is quite separate from anorexia and bulimia. Rumination, the chewing of regurgitated food in the mouth is on occasion part of the anorexic or bulimic picture but rarely appears in the literature. Another form of eating disorder which, as yet, has not made its way into the psychiatric textbooks is 'spitting', where food is chewed, but not swallowed. It is spat out into available receptacles, from bowls and loos to tissues and hands.

The current diagnostic criteria for anorexia are:

A. Refusal to maintain body weight over a minimal normal weight for age and height, for example, weight loss leading to maintenance of body weight 15 per cent below that expected; or failure to make expected weight gain during period of growth, leading to body weight 15 per cent below that expected.

B. Intense fear of gaining weight or becoming fat, even though underweight.

C. Disturbance in the way in which one's body weight, size, or shape is experienced, for example, the person claims to 'feel fat' even when emaciated, believes that one area of the body is 'too fat' even when obviously underweight.

D. In females, absence of at least three consecutive menstrual cycles when otherwise expected to occur (primary or secondary amenorrhea). (A woman is considered to have amenorrhea if her periods occur only following hormone – for example, estrogen – administration.) (*DSM-III-R*, p. 67)

Bulimic symptoms of self-induced vomiting, the taking of laxatives and diuretics, are referred to in the general description. They are not diagnostic criteria, since not all anorexics suffer from them, but many do. The point is made that individuals can have both anorexia and bulimia. Other generally observed features of anorexic behaviour are excessive exercising, a wish to feed others, often with elaborate meals, and the secret hoarding of food.

Women still make up the majority of anorexics, up to 95 per cent. Anorexia can be fatal, and between 5 and 18 per cent of sufferers die as a result of the illness.

The current diagnostic criteria for bulimia nervosa are:

A. Recurrent episodes of binge eating (rapid consumption of a large amount of food in a discrete period of time).
B. A feeling of lack of control over eating behaviour during the eating binges.
C. The person regularly engages in either self-induced vomiting, use of laxatives or diuretics, strict dieting or fasting, or vigorous exercise in order to prevent weight gain.
D. A minimum average of two binge eating episodes a week for at least three months.
E. Persistent over-concern with body shape and weight.
(*DSM-III-R*, p. 69)

Bingeing is not described in the general category of anorexic behaviour, although it is implied. Bulimics are described as generally bingeing on easily consumed, high calorific food: 'The food is usually gobbled down quite rapidly, with little chewing' (*DSM-III-R*, p. 67). Binges come to an end due to discomfort, sleep, interruptions or self-induced vomiting. (In practice this is usually when the available food has run out.) Sometimes vomiting is the desired goal: 'Although eating binges may be pleasurable, disparaging self-criticism and a depressed mood often follow ... Often these people feel that their life is dominated by conflicts about eating' (*DSM-III-R*, p. 67). Vomiting is listed as one of the ways in which food is dealt with, suggesting that individuals who binge and then exercise or diet to get rid of it are bulimic. For the purposes of my work I consider bulimics to be those who binge and vomit or take inappropriately large numbers of laxatives. I would view non-vomiters or laxative takers as being compulsive eaters or possibly sufferers of SED.

According to *DSM-III-R*, features which are at times associated with bulimia are drug taking, depression and borderline personality disorder. It is stated that the usual course of the illness is chronic and intermittent, although the time span of these respective states is not described. Bulimia is not usually incapacitating. It can be if all day is spent bingeing, vomiting and taking laxatives. There are weight fluctuations, but these are rarely so extreme as to threaten life – although what may threaten life are cardiac arrhythmias as a result of an electrolyte imbalance.

The similarities and differences may be seen as falling into four categories: attitudes to eating, body image concerns, actual effects on the body and other psychological and emotional features. Anorexics eat little and fear losing control; bulimics do lose control. Both groups fear putting on weight and becoming fat, although anorexics are already thin. Anorexics have amenorrhea. Bulimics usually do not, although they misuse their bodies by self-induced vomiting and/or by taking laxatives and diuretics. Anorexics have a high mortality rate; whereas bulimics are seldom in danger of losing their lives. The issue of life or death is explicitly more relevant for anorexics. Some anorexics suffer from obsessive–compulsive disorder. Bulimics may suffer from depression, addictions or borderline personality disorder, suggesting a greater breadth of psychological disturbance.

Comparing the different pictures of the symptoms described, anorexia and bulimia are not the same illness. A major anomaly is that bulimics, by definition, have to be within a normal weight range, and yet a person can be both bulimic and anorexic at the same time, thus disregarding the relevance of one of the symptoms which differentiates between the two disorders. This is the confusion. The obvious answer would seem to be to create three rather than two groups so that the weight distinction can be preserved. Following this line of thought, there would be restrictor anorexics, bulimic anorexics and normal weight bulimics. From now on I shall use the term 'anorexics' to refer to restrictor anorexics, 'anorexic bulimics' or 'bulimic anorexics' to refer to themselves and bulimics to refer to normal weight bulimics. I have decided not to use Marlene Boskind-White and William C. White's term 'bulimarexia', first coined by them in 1975 (Boskind-White and White, 1987, pp. 19–20) to refer to bingers and purgers or Russell's 1979 term 'bulimia nervosa'. Neither term is used consistently in the literature, and although Boskind-White and White claim that Russell's term is exactly equivalent to theirs, they do not have weight as a defining characteristic, whereas Russell does, and wants to use 'bulimia nervosa' to describe anorexic bulimics, not normal weight bulimics. It is for ease of recognition and clarity that I have decided to use the terms outlined above.

It is clear that bulimics use their bodies in quite a different way from restrictor anorexics (those who do not have symptoms of bingeing and vomiting) and perhaps from anorexic bulimics, and this may reflect different unconscious phantasies, both in general and in particular. I want to look at the emergence of these disorders over time to further elucidate their relationship to each other, how the symptoms have been described and how they have been understood, before moving on to the implications for working psychotherapeutically with these patients.

The most obvious change – and one that needs addressing immediately – is that 'anorexia' is a misnomer. Etymologically, anorexia means absence of desire. But anorexia is not about not having an appetite. When Gull (1873) and Lasègue (1873) coined the term, the notion of starvation being undertaken voluntarily was an idea that was simply not considered. Anorexia was, at that time, understood as an illness where the appetite vanished. The desperate awareness and fear of hunger that anorexics experience was not recognised. It was kept secret by the sufferers and was not linked by their carers to the outbreak of bulimic symptoms.

George Gilles de la Tourette (1895) understood the ravenous and terrifying nature of the hunger that his patients experienced, and by the 1940s this denial of hunger was increasingly connected to a fear of becoming fat. The unconscious understanding of the symptomology of anorexia and bulimia, from the late nineteenth century onwards, could certainly be understood in this context. It is but a small step from the wish to be thin to the fear of being fat. Pierre Janet (1929) tells of a patient of Charcot's who wore a rose ribbon around her waist which she would not untie. She was not to get any larger. The fear of becoming fat was seen as the motive for not eating, and not eating was thought of as being a defence against the terror of a gargantuan, destructive and overwhelming appetite. The emphasis on the fear of becoming fat by clinicians has added a vital piece of understanding to the anorexic jigsaw which remains firmly in place with the work of Wilson *et al.* (1985, 1992).

The term 'anorexia' came to the minds of two men at much the same time. In 1868 William Withey Gull, an English surgeon, and Charles Lasègue in France were – unaware of each other – both working with anorexics. They decided independently on the name of anorexia, after a number of others had been mooted and then discarded. 'Hysterical anorexia' had been put forward by Lasègue but was then dropped when it became clear that not all anorexics had an hysterical character structure. Gull pointed out that hysteria was a diagnosis given only to women at that time, and not all anorexics were female.

The search for normal weight bulimics, according to *DSM-III-R* immediately runs into trouble – but for very different reasons. The etymological route gives a fair description of one half of the bulimic picture, but only half. Bulimia comes from the Greek words *bous* meaning ox and *lipos* meaning hunger. The historians of psychiatry, Parry-Jones and Parry Jones commented:

> The *Oxford English Dictionary* (1961), under the heading *bulimy*, provides four examples of the use of the term, from 1651 to 1780, with consistent presentation of the condition as a state of insatiability and dog-like appetite. (1991, p. 130)

If bulimia is exclusively about 'ox-like hunger' then compulsive eaters should be termed bulimic. In fact historical data on normal weight bulimics, who both binge and get rid of the food, has simply not been found. What is described in reported cases of bulimia, such as those described by Parry Jones, tends to be behaviour which is closer to the psychotic end of the spectrum and is often shocking and exhibitionistic. What may be skewing the picture is the element of secrecy in bulimic behaviour. This is not mentioned in the *DSM* but is apparent from the presenting descriptions in the consulting room, because bulimic behaviour, excessive overeating and vomiting and/or laxative taking is usually done behind closed doors. Although, in the United States it has been noted as a passing phenomenon among groups of college students, the majority of whom do not go on to develop a formal eating disorder (Hogan, 1992). It also occurs in the United Kingdom in a number of private day schools for girls (Felton, 1994).

Historically, we are left with the development of anorexia nervosa as a syndrome which does in practice include a description and understanding of anorexic bulimics – who are very low weight *and* binge and vomit – although they are not separated in the literature. Bulimic behaviour, as either part of, or separate from, anorexia has been described by Gull (1873), MacKensie (1888), Osler (1892), Soltman (1894), Abraham (1916), Stunkard, Grace and Woff (1955), Bruch (1962), Thöma (1967), Sperling (1978), Casper, Eckert, Halmi, Goldberg and Davis (1980), Wilson (1982), Wilson *et al.* (1985) and others. Clear distinctions between the two have not been made.

I shall look at the emergence of anorexia and, whenever possible, at normal weight bulimia (but the scarcity and lack of clarity in the material makes this difficult), and I shall consider four main themes. The first is the gradual emergence of an emotional and psychological mode of understanding anorexic and bulimic symptoms, in preference to a biological and physiological one. Secondly, I shall explore these meanings as understood psychoanalytically, giving particular attention to Freudian, post-Freudian and Kleinian approaches. Thirdly, I wish to explore Winnicott's ideas on transitional phenomena in relation to the body and the behaviour of an individual with bulimic symptoms. Finally, I shall look at the difficulties of working with these patients in the consulting room. I shall suggest that an understanding of Kleinian narcissism and the concept of transitional objects can perhaps point a way forward in the technique used with these individuals which might enable them to take in and digest both the therapeutic atmosphere and interpretations.

CHAPTER 2

Psychoanalytic Understandings

Beginnings

Sours, unlike other historians of eating disorders, suggests evidence can be found for anorexia as early as the eleventh century. He refers to Avicenna, a Persian physician and philosopher, who treated a young prince who had anorexic symptoms and melancholia. His delusional system was successfully broken through, and he recovered (Sours 1980, p. 205). Rudolph Bell in *Holy Anorexia* makes a convincing case that Catherine of Sienna (1347–80) was anorexic, if not anorexic bulimic. She made herself vomit, although she did not apparently eat large amounts of food. Bell is sensitive to, and aware of the dangers he faces in such an enquiry, not only in terms of the different cultural, societal and psychological influences, but also because of the very nature of the material which he is dealing with. Whether the 'holy women' of the thirteenth to fifteenth century did suffer from bulimic anorexia is still being debated, (Bell, 1985; Bynum, 1987) not only because of Bell's uncertainties, but because of an argument, put forward by Brumberg, that the symptom of restricted eating was only one component of a complex pattern of behaviour, which included violence directed towards the self (Brumberg, 1988). This presupposes that such behaviour is not part of the experience of late twentieth century anorexics and bulimic anorexics. However, self harm is part of the behaviour of some anorexics and anorexic bulimics. It may take the form of self-mutilation, burning, cutting, scratching, over-exercising (which can lead to severe joint problems), laxative, diuretic or other drug abuse. There are many different ways of inducing vomiting, from a simple clenching of the stomach muscles to the use of knives and other objects – even fingernails may damage the back of the throat, and the knuckles of the hands may be scraped by the teeth. There is certainly no doubt that these medieval women fasted, vomited, were overactive and had amenorrhea. They also gained political power and prestige by their actions (once they had convinced those around them that they were neither witches, nor possessed by the devil). Questions concerning the degree of body image distortion, the wish to remain thin and the fear of becoming fat are all unanswerable. What was clear was the subjugation of the flesh and a desire for spirituality and otherworldliness which was to be achieved through starvation and the physical destruction of the body. Many anorexics and anorexic bulimics wish to destroy their bodies and yet preserve the fantasy of continued existence (Bruch, 1978; Palazzoli, 1978). In this way a link is clear. The fantasy of immortality is as true for some anorexics in the twentieth century as it was for those in the fifteenth century. 'Death becomes a logical, sweet and total liberation from the flesh' (Bell, 1985, p. 13). Bell is writing about Catherine of Sienna, but the same words might well have applied to Catherine Dunbar, an anorexic who starved herself to death in 1983 (Dunbar, 1987).

What has changed is how eating disorders are understood. The meaning of the symptom of self-starvation has shifted in society's eyes. Psychotherapists view these thoughts as being psychotic delusions, while for the 'holy women' they were the source of the prestige and power they had in their society. In the 1990s the context of religious fanaticism is not a feature of anorexia, but physical fanaticism is – not only among anorexics and bulimics. Some individuals become severely addicted to exercise and the control they have over their body. Many women with whom I have worked would like a 'touch' of anorexia. These may be women attending workshops on food and eating, fellow psychotherapists and friends. Reports in the media suggest many are willing to pay high prices for an ideal and young body – an idea taken to extremes in Robert Zemeckis' 1993 film, *Death Becomes Her*, where women keep their youthful bodies at the expense of immortality. They never die. Young women are one of the fastest growing group of new smokers. The wish to restrict their eating and their appetite is a large and accepted part of their motivation (*Evening Standard*, 25 November 1993). Plastic surgery, liposuction and the prescription of drugs to speed up the metabolism, as well as the multi-million pound business of diet food, drinks and books, suggests most of us share in the unconscious phantasy of a perfect body leading to a perfect life.

Symptoms

The presence or absence of unconscious rather than conscious death wish phantasies cannot be worked out in retrospect in relation to medieval female religious fanatics. The symptom picture is not clear enough, and their families, lives and individual histories cannot substitute for working with an individual psychodynamically. The impact, influence and effect of their culture and their society on them as individuals is also hard to determine. From the time of Morton (1689) onwards, a clear and relatively stable symptom picture of anorexia has existed. Surprisingly little has changed over time, although some shifts have occurred between the categories, and some symptoms have left the diagnostic picture altogether, but this does not mean they are not clinically in evidence. Morton, in his *Pathisologica or a Treatise on Consumption*, written in 1689, documented two cases of anorexia and described them as 'a nervous atrophy, a consumption of mental origin, without fever or dyspepsia, with the symptomology of food avoidance, amenorrhea, lack of appetite, constipation, extreme emaciation, and over activity' (p. 206). He recognised the mental origin, the severe weight loss, amenorrhea and overactivity. This symptom picture remained constant over the next two hundred years or so. Some clinicians noticed the presence of vomiting in their patients and some did not. Lasègue was criticised for failing to recognise the primacy of amenorrhea. He also dismissed the presence of vomiting in the anorexics he saw. 'There is neither vomiting nor any real desire to vomit even in extreme cases, the patient only asserting that a degree beyond would induce this' (Lasègue, 1873, pp. 146–7). Most recognised the non-physical nature of the disorder and the powerful influence of the mother on the patient.

Bulimic symptoms were recognised from early on, as was binge eating – but what was not seen was the distortion of body image and the fear of becoming fat that informs so much of how eating disorders are understood today. Starving was not connected to bingeing. Sollier (1891) and Charcot (1889) both recognised a desire to be thin – one half of the fear of becoming fat – in anorexics, but Gilles de la Tourette was the first clinician to recognise that although sufferers refused to eat, there was no loss of appetite – rather it was perceptions of food and the body which were distorted. He was the first to correct the misnomer of anorexia; he rechristened it 'anorexia gastrique'.

From the late nineteenth century onwards attempts were made to understand anorexia in terms of physical illness. Both Gull and Lasègue initially attempted to find a physical cause for anorexia. In reports in the *Lancet* Gull linked it to a gastric nervous malfunction, and similarly Lasègue (1873) believed it was related to a malfunction of the gastrointestinal tract. The presence or absence of constipation as a symptom of anorexia does not have the relevance which it had in the late nineteenth and early twentieth centuries, although peculiar eating habits, or non-habits do affect the digestive tract, as does the psychological state of the patient. The intestinal focus on constipation in anorexics has perhaps been supplanted by an interest in the taking of laxatives and diuretics by anorexic bulimics and bulimics, which causes diarrhoea and can lead to severe constipation and permanent damage of the gastrointestinal tract. Whether this has taken place cannot be determined until the abuse of laxatives is discontinued. The symbolic meaning or the frequency of the taking of enemas in the context of eating disorders has not been explored, but physically the delicate balance of the gastrointestinal tract can be adversely effected by this procedure. Constipation, bloating and chronic wind are seen more as symptoms of recovery once eating has been resumed, rather than as part of the primary picture, among the bulimic groups.

The complex interaction between eating behaviour, physical symptoms and psychological and emotional states was dispensed with by many when Maurice Simmonds, a pathologist at St George's Hospital in Hamburg, suggested that emaciation could be the result of pituitary destruction or deficiency (Simmonds, 1914, 1916). For the next twenty years many anorexics were diagnosed as suffering from panhypopituitarism and were treated with extracts from the pituitary gland. Simmonds' findings were misleading and meant that by 1916 most cases of anorexia were treated as physical disorders. The concept of Simmonds' disease was challenged in the 1930s:

> In 1936, Ryle demonstrated that psychosexual trauma could lead to amenorrhea. His psycho-endocrine thesis was further elaborated by Reifenstien in 1946, when the latter described several cases of amenorrhea demonstrably due to psychophysiological causes. This research clearly established that developmental traumas and interferences, as well as psychosocial stress, can alter hormone patterns and secretions and led to a burgeoning of interest in the psychobiology of anorexia nervosa. (Sours, 1980, p. 210)

This discovery led to a renewed search for understanding the links between anorexia, the individual and society, although the dehumanisation of eating disorder patients and their symptoms is a trend that chillingly continues today:

> The investigation of structural brain abnormalities in patients with bulimia nervosa is a continuing topic of current psychiatric research ... Research by Lautenbacher, Galfe, Hoelzl and Prike (1989) on similar lines, revealed delayed gastrointestinal transit in a sample of patients with bulimia. (Parry Jones and Parry Jones, 1991, p. 140)

Alternative Psychoanalytic Understandings of Symptoms

Eating disorders may be seen as psychosomatic illnesses; indeed, Kaufman and Heiman see anorexia as paradigmatic in *Evolution of Psychosomatic Concepts. Anorexia Nervosa: A Paradigm*, which they edited in 1964. This does not, however, alter the basic question: how are symptoms described, and what are the meanings that are attached to them? The bulk of the literature on eating disorders originates in the United States where the majority of therapists are ego psychologists, following on in the tradition of Anna Freud, as interpreted by Kris (1950), Lowenstein (1951), Hartman (1958), and Rappaport (1960). The two main groups represented in working with eating disorders are those who use a conflictual model (Sperling, 1978; Wilson *et al.*, 1985, 1992) and those who follow a Kohutian deficit model (Goodsitt, 1983, 1985; Swift and Letven, 1984). For the former group, a symptom 'is viewed as the end product of a complex developmental series of childhood wishes and fantasies, and defensive transfigurations and revision' (Schwartz, 1988a, p. 36). It remains firmly in the hands of the instincts, particularly the sex drive. According to the ego psychologists a symptom represents a repressed wish and denial of that wish, as can be seen with Freud's understanding of hysterical vomiting quoted below. For Kohut and his followers, however, eating disorders are understood as a way to supply missing self-object functions (Brenner, 1983; Geist, 1985; Gehrie, 1990; Sands, 1991). In many ways this comes close to an object relations approach, and is a very persuasive way of working with eating disordered patients. Susan Sand's paper on 'Bulimia, Dissociation and Empathy: A Self-Psychological View' (1991) is extremely clear and persuasive, but its emphasis seems to me to fail to give due attention to the violence of the unconscious phantasies of patients and to the importance of coming to terms with adult sexuality and some kind of a working through of the Oedipal situation.

I shall look at the understandings of bulimia and anorexia from these points of view before moving on to an object relations approach as understood by the Kleinian school, where the symptom is seen as occurring within, and emerging as part of a phantasy (fantasy with a 'ph' always meaning it is unconscious) of an internal object relationship. Accordingly, a symptom is understood as being an expression of an object relationship, rather than being set off by sexual or aggressive drives, although aggression and sexuality may well feature among other emotions in the complicated nature of the exchange. This way of understanding anorexic and bulimic symptoms anchors them in the primitive internal world of object relations, unconscious phantasy, primitive anxieties and pathological narcissism that Kleinians believe occur from birth onwards, unlike the ego psychologists, for whom object relations do not occur until nine months or so (Mahler *et al.*, 1975).

Although the ego psychologists call anorexia a psychosomatic illness, their Oedipal and libidinal understanding of the symptom suggests they see it as conversion hysteria. This is strongly refuted by Christopher Dare: 'Psychosomatic symptoms are not hysterical conversions; the elucidation of the fantasies with which the physical symptoms are associated in the patient's mind do not reliably provide relief from the symptoms' (1993, p. 12). Despite these objections, a great deal of work on understanding anorexic and bulimic symptoms has been explored in terms of a regression from the Oedipus complex – both positive and negative – and it is this territory that I shall look at first.

Pre-Freudian

Prior to the development of psychoanalytic ways of thinking, it was acknowledged that anorexia was an illness whose origins lay in feelings and the mind, rather than being biologically determined. As we have seen, Morton, as early as 1689, not only provided an accurate description of anorexic symptomology but also recognised its psychological origins. Gull (1873) and Lasègue (1873) moved from a purely biological to a psychological understanding. As Kaufman and Heiman have observed, 'Lasègue was so impressed with psychological factors in control of appetite that he tried to explain even the voraciousness of the diabetic as being of psychological origin' (1964, p. 142).

From the late eighteenth century, the psychological influence of the mother was seen as being a major, although rather mysterious, part of the problem (Nandeau, 1789; Gull, 1873; Lasègue, 1873; Charcot, 1889). The historical emergence of the primacy of the mother–child relationship and the relevance of the pathology of the mother is explored in more detail in the next chapter.

Classical Freudians

Freud (1899), Osler (1912) and Riddle (1914) took a different tack and linked bulimic symptoms of food cravings and vomiting to hysteria, which, despite Gull and Lasègue's earlier objections, continued to be seen as the aetiology of anorexia. In his *Three Essays on the Theory of Sexuality* Freud brings nourishment and sexuality firmly together; they are only separated once weaning occurs. He says of the first psycho-sexual phase, the oral phase:

> The first of these is the oral or, as it might be called, cannibalistic pregenital sexual organization. Here sexual activity has not yet been separated from the ingestion of food; nor are opposite currents within the activity differentiated. The object of both activities is the same; the sexual aim consists in the incorporation of the object – the prototype of a process which, in the form of identification, is later to play such an important psychological part. (Freud, 1905, p. 337)

The possible divergence of two lines of thought about the meaning of symptoms can be traced from this quote. Does the taking in of nourishment remain for eating disorder patients a sexually driven activity, or is it a prototype of a way of object relating based on introjective identification, or is it both?

Freud refers to hysterical vomiting in his case history of Dora and in a letter to Fliess.

> Because in phantasy she is pregnant, because she is so insatiable that she cannot put up with not having a baby by her last phantasy-lover as well. But she must vomit too because in that case she will be starved and emaciated, and will lose her beauty and no longer be attractive to

anyone. Thus the sense of the symptom is a contradictory pair of wish-fulfilments. (Freud, 1899, p. 278)

It is clear that he does not view it as being a fixation at the oral stage but rather as a defensive regression against positive Oedipal wishes.

Freud recognised the displacement of genital wishes to the mouth and the unconscious existence of the mouth–vagina equation. Jones (1927) went one step further and recognised the mouth–anus–vagina equation. These conceptualisations, particularly the former, have been used by many as a template to understand anorexia and bulimia throughout the twentieth century (Greenacre, 1950, 1952; Fraiberg, 1972; Sperling, 1973).

> The transformation of a conflict on the genital level to a conflict on an oral basis is part of the ego's effort to gain mastery over a genital conflict by a change of venue, so to speak, by shifting the struggle to a safer, more familiar and more controllable ground. (Ritvo, 1984, p. 454)

It provides an accessible route to one way of understanding anorexia as being a defence against a wish for impregnation.

Post-Freud

Following Freud's earlier reasonings, Waller, Kaufman and Deutsch, in a classic paper, elaborated in much greater detail the nature of the particular oral phantasy which they felt was present in anorexia: 'Anorexics have psychological factors that have a specific constellation centring around the symbolization of pregnancy fantasies involving the gastrointestinal tract' (Waller, Kaufman and Deutsch, 1940, p. 260). Their understanding is also of relevance to anorexic bulimics and to those normal weight bulimics who do have amenorrhea.

> We see then, a syndrome the main symptoms of which represent an elaboration and acting out in the somatic sphere of a specific type of fantasy. The wish to be impregnated through the mouth which results, at times, in compulsive eating, and at other times, in guilt and

consequent rejection of food, the constipation symbolizing the child in the abdomen and the amenorrhea as the direct psychological repercussion of pregnancy fantasies. This amenorrhea may also be part of the direct denial of genital sexuality. (p. 272)

The complicated nature of the defences, displacements and hidden gratification of wishes is well described by Schwartz.

> To the child and the unconscious, food is the paternal phallus, ingestion of which undoes castration and conceives the oedipal baby (Waller *et al.*, 1940, Lorand, 1943; Leonard, 1944; Sylvester, 1945; Blos, 1974). The incorporative act of eating–gorging contains the desire for abdominal distension and impregnation, the defence of upward displacement with oral submission to mother, and the punishment of physical revulsion. The expulsive act of vomiting desexualises the receptive wish, symbolically rejects and restores the ingested phallus-baby, sadistically punishes the thwarting object, and masochistically relieves the guilt evoked by the desire to castrate and possess father (Masserman, 1941; Leonard, 1944; Kestenberg, 1968). (Schwartz, 1988a, p. 39)

To Have a Penis?

Following this line of thought, the question then arises as to the role of father's penis and what it means in phantasy for the female child to have a penis. Is it a wish for a baby from father, which is unconsciously meant to equal a penis, as in the classical understanding of the positive Oedipus complex? Or is it about wishing to have a penis, to identify with the masculine, in effect, to take up what Freud referred to as the negative Oedipal position, a position developmentally prior to the positive Oedipal position? If it is positive, then the wish to replace mother and have a child from father is paramount. If it is negative, the anorexic, or bulimic, identifies with the father and wishes to compete phallically with him for the possession and sexual control of mother (Lampl-de Groot, 1927; Deutsch, 1930, 1932,

1944, 1945; Freud, 1931; Brunswick, 1940; Nagera, 1975). Masserman gives an example of such a patient whose fantasies centred around the acquisition of a penis. She had her periods but was of a relatively low weight, and binged and vomited; she was probably a bulimic:

> At this time the material also began to deal with the specific nature of her incorporative desires toward men, namely, to acquire their penises as a symbol of the masculinity desired by her mother and thereby eliminate them as competitors and displace them homosexually in her mother's affections. (Masserman, 1941, p. 330)

In *Psychoanalytic Theories of Development: An Integration* Tyson and Tyson (1990) suggest that not all girls go through the negative Oedipal complex prior to a positive one as Freud thought. They have argued that if it occurs, it occurs after the positive stage and suggests disturbed object relations based on wanting to control mother and deny triangulation. Prophecy Coles links this point to perversion:

> I believe Freud was correct when he said some girls are unable to face the unpalatable fact that they have no penis. They continue to enact their 'masculine life' and maintain their original relationship to their mother because their rage against her is too great. In this refusal to give up their 'masculine life' we see a sexualisation of aggression that is both intense and compelling. (Coles, 1988, p. 146)

This suggests there may be a refusal to acknowledge the presence and potency of father in relation to both self and mother. His separateness and his function as part of a copulating couple is to be denied.

To Be a Penis?

Bearing the presence of identification with a masculine ideal in mind, Abraham (1924) suggested that the body itself, by its very thinness, becomes identified with the penis. This idea was taken a step further by Lewin (1933), who saw vomiting as being a partial identification with an ejaculating, urinating phallus. Sperling (1983), Wilson (1983) and Sarnoff (1983)

saw the flat stomach of the anorexic as being a retreat to a
phallic ideal, which was a defence against the feminine wish
to be made pregnant by father in phantasy and therefore having
to compete with mother. Masserman (1941) and Leonard
(1944) both described as central the conflicts of assuming a
female role. Schwartz (1988b) is one of the few authors who
distinguishes between anorexics and normal weight bulimics.
He makes the point that although normal weight bulimics
have masculine identifications and ideals, they recognise
that they do not have a penis, however much they may want
one. He contrasts this to anorexics, who by their starving
become a penis in phantasy so doing away with father, or the
need for a man altogether. This suggests that the distinction
is between wishing to compete with father in order to replace
him in mother's bed and affections by having a penis, as
Masserman (1941) thought, or omnipotently wishing to
control mother by becoming a penis, in effect eliminating all
knowledge of father and the possibility of triangulation.

To Avoid Being Either a Man or a Woman

This confusion of gender identity and the possibility of
simultaneously holding two positions is reminiscent of
Aristophanes, who suggested that originally there were three
sexes, not two. There were not only men and women but
also a man and a woman combined. In my clinical experience
many bulimics and anorexics attempt to postpone indefinitely
the realisation of which sex they belong to, as though it was
a decision that could be made by choice alone. They attempt
to identify with being both male and female and so imagine
they can provide everything for themselves. A retreat into
this particular form of narcissism can be seen in some
patients, whereas in others an earlier form seems to be
present, where the very knowledge of a separate existence
from mother is not allowed to reach consciousness. I shall
return to this later. As Harvey Schwartz has suggested:

> Thus, the stereotyped ritual of gorging on food and
> forcing one's finger down the throat to induce regurgi-
> tation represents in part a simultaneous identification with

both parents of the primal scene with an acting out on one's own body of the imagined role of the sadistic phallic father and castrated suffering mother. This defensive bisexual identification denies the humiliation of primal-scene exclusion, undoes 'castration' and reverses passive (masochistic) oedipal impregnation wishes. (1988a, p. 40)

Alternating identification with one parent and the other has been reported by Karol (1980) in regard to asthma patients. Both Moulton (1942) and Sperling (1983) recognised the masturbatory aspect of the bulimic ritual.

Not Oedipal but Pre-Oedipal

This seems to suggest that what matters is being in charge, in control of both parents. No freedom or creativity between self and a parent, or between parents, is allowed. The problems of the unresolved pre-Oedipal relationship to the mother becomes explosive in relation to mother and father during adolescence. It is not just about having sexual intercourse, but is also about how anorexics and bulimics perceive their role and others in relationships. The interest of many clinicians from Jessner and Abse (1960) to Palazzoli (1978), Sprince (1984), Boris (1984a, 1984b, 1988), Mushatt (1992) and Wilson (1992a), moved from looking at anorexic and bulimic behaviour as representing repressed sexual and aggressive drives at an Oedipal level, to looking at the much earlier pre-Oedipal mother–child relationship. This paralleled a shift from drives to looking at what bulimic and anorexic symptoms were representing in terms of very early object relationships, where the mode of relating is based on control and survival (in Kleinian terms the powerful feelings of the paranoid–schizoid position).

The concrete nature of the thought of bulimics and anorexics and their omnipotent wish to control important objects in their lives is clear in some of their reported fantasies. Maguire noted, 'On the one hand, she wanted to come between them and have exclusive possession of each. She couldn't, she insisted, face the idea of her mother or myself being part of a sexual couple. "It makes me feel ill"'(1989, p. 118).

This is graphically illustrated by a male patient, who imagined being in his parents' bed 'lying between them, with his father's penis in his rectum, and his own penis in his mother's rectum – a blissful state of complete union and sole possession of both parents' (Mushatt, 1992, p. 304). I would disagree with Mushatt: far from blissful, this fantasy could be construed as hopeless, claustrophobic, immobilising and omnipotent – illustrating the perverse desire to deny separation, sexual difference and triangular relationships.

We are getting further and further from classical thoughts on the Oedipus complex and nearer to a recognition that perhaps the difficulties are more accurately portrayed as being part of the mother–daughter relationship. The scenes above are not apparently about reproductive sexuality; they are about control, power and immobility, rather than creativity. Palazzoli wrote, 'The sexual problem is not the basic one. All my women patients were fixated at the pre-genital levels' (1978, p. 76). The Kleinian understanding of part objects and Oedipal relationships creates a soup rather than a linear developmental path, with oral, anal, phallic and genital overlapping and interlocking in ever-fluctuating combinations.

The lack of differentiation between self and mother and vice-versa is the basis for understanding both anorexia and bulimia. This is, of course, a description of Klein's (1946) narcissistic state. The focus has moved from oral impregnation fantasies to failures to achieve adequate separation–individuation from mother. This narcissistic difficulty means, in turn, that negotiating Oedipal issues – whether they be seen in a Freudian or Kleinian light – is going to be problematic for these patients.

Problems of Separation–Individuation

The eating disordered individual's relationship to her mother has been strangely absent from the story up to now. Penises and pregnancy phantasies, wishing to replace father or to have or become a penis have been examined. The child's earlier relationship to mother has been in the background, not the foreground, yet eating may not be a substitute for the penis, or for a baby: it may be about eating. Eating originally was about eating mother and not knowing where mother began and baby ended. To understand something of object relations we need to go back to the beginning where symbolic equations reigned unopposed: food = mother and mother = food. The concrete nature of this statement is where the trouble starts. Before a baby can become separate from mother he or she has to recognise that mother is other than herself or himself. Kleinian theory suggests that from birth onwards we have phantasies – unconscious ones, many layered and multitudinous, stemming from our experiences of our bodies – and this colours how we understand and expect to relate in the real world. We begin by having extremely good and extremely bad phantasies about our mother's body, bits and pieces of it. In the baby's mind these experiences are split into two, good experiences and bad experiences, or put another way, an excellent mother who meets our needs and a vicious angry mother who abandons us and does not meet our needs. In phantasy there are two separate people: one whom we have to protect ourselves from in order to survive, the other who provides us with all we need and could ever want.

According to Kleinian theory destructive impulses of our own are projected into mother in order to be rid of these painful and difficult feelings. Mother, in phantasy, then becomes furious and potentially retaliatory. The filter becomes an angry and destructive one. Waller *et al.*, (1940), Lorand (1943) and Hogan (1992) suggest that the Oedipal castration wishes are so strong due to the intensity of the child's early oral struggles and the strength of their sadism and aggression. This can be understood as suggesting the proliferation of violent, destroying and destructive internal part-object relationships, at the level of unconscious phantasy. What is vital for successful development is the predominance of good experiences over bad ones, so that when it is realised that mother is but one person, a good and bad mother, good prevails internally. The emergence of concern for the other person surfaces as the good has to be protected from the bad.

This is the depressive position. Survival as *the* aim is superseded. For this to occur, good experiences have to have been allowed and to have been successfully taken in the first place. Kleinians believe that we carry an internal picture of the world, full of part and whole objects to which we relate, and it is this picture, this unconscious filter, through which we see and experience the world and every situation with which we come in contact.

Anorexic behaviour has been understood as being about pathological narcissism, where not only is mother not recognised as being separate from the child, but she is thought to have nothing to offer. Primary envy is seen as so pernicious that it destroys all knowledge, awareness of a good breast, because knowledge of it would mean recognition of something good outside of the person themselves, which would be intolerable. This is how anorexic and bulimic behaviour is understood by Boris (1984a, 1984b, 1988). Anorexics become omnipotent in order to survive, as the knowledge of there being anything good which is not in their possession is unbearable. The breast is rubbished until there is little that could be got from it. Instead 'less' becomes 'more', to avoid wanting becomes the clue to existence. To have others want, to be devoid of desire is the aim: to be anorexic. In phantasy, 'no needs' means no separation, for being entirely self-sufficient prevents any awareness of dependency needs in relation to the self. If desire does not exist, mother unconsciously need not exist. The connection of both birth and early nurturing and dependence can be denied. Unconsciously, for many anorexics food still concretely equals mother. Food is the substitute for a longing for fusion, a longing for mother. If the desire was known, then the only result would be enslavement to mother and food. By starving it need never be known. Implicit in Boris's idea of an anorexic's internal world is the presence of a mother who enslaves, who does not want to be separate from her child and cannot bear to know about her neediness. I will return to this later.

Sohn sees it somewhat differently, implying that all connections are likely to fail because envy must not be experienced, yet paradoxically connections and links are continually sought but must never be found:

> To my mind, there is a form of envy, which operates by promoting unawareness of the source of pleasure and of pleasure itself so as to be defended against an awareness of envy. The enjoyment giving object is then neither recognised properly nor separated from. Nor will the specificity of the object be noticed or acknowledged, which leads to further strange searchings for a possible repetition. (Sohn, 1985, p. 51)

What is being put forward is that anorexics and bulimics cannot separate from their mothers as their envy of the breast is too great, that to know of this envy would destroy them and their mother, and so in phantasy they possess, control or become mother. An excess of envy is so powerful in Kleinian thought that it prevents the necessary splitting into very good and very bad that is essential for early object relating and growth. Nothing good can be tolerated. There is, I think, something missing here. Unconscious envy may be an element in the difficulties anorexic and bulimic women experience, as may extreme destructive feelings, but by *only* looking through the filter of the child, the impact of the movements, feelings and actions of the mother seem to fade into relative insignificance. This is not to deny the existence of envy and profound destructive feelings in these patients. What we have to do in order to present a more balanced picture is to enter the arena of muddle between mother and child, where who is who is uncertain. To lay the blame on innate envy or on the mother is neither appropriate nor helpful. The complicated nature of the entwined relationship of mother and child is what needs to be looked at if work with these patients is to be productive.

The bewildering nature of apparently self-destructive omnipotence has already been noted among medieval religious martyrs. Can wilful starvation be understood? Normal weight bulimics rarely suffer from the severity of body image distortion which anorexics and anorexic bulimics do (Schwartz, 1988b). They rarely die. Death is much lower down their unconscious agenda, although the incidence of conscious depression and suicidal inclinations is much higher in this group. Are anorexics actually trying to kill themselves? Charcot thought so in 1889, as did Janet in 1929 and Lorand in 1943. Janet believed it was a response to a rejection, while Charcot and Lorand clearly attributed it to something that was taking place in the mother–daughter interaction, as did Nandeau, some hundred years earlier in 1789. What it was that was deleterious in the mother–daughter relationship was not explored. Palazzoli (1978) thought that anorexics identified their physical selves with the bad mother, who then threatened to destroy or overwhelm them from within when they ate. Starvation was for them a way of attempting to avoid, deny and control the bad mother. Yet because of the paranoid–schizoid state they were in, they forgot – were blind to – the impossibility of starving mother without starving themselves. Joyce McDougall, in her book *Theatres of the Body*, speaks of a patient with severe psychosomatic symptoms who believed that by physically damaging her body she could concretely disprove the belief that her body was her mother's body, and if she separated from it she would die (1989, p. 141). Cecil Mushatt sees it differently:

> There are instances when the rejection of food expresses the fantasy of omnipotence and invulnerability because of the unconscious fantasy of complete union with mother. Because of this symbolic fantasy, there is no need to eat. To eat food is to acknowledge the fact of separation and of one's mortal being. (1992, p. 309)

Death simply does not exist. Yet it does. This is an alternative understanding of no needs meaning no separation, as described in Harold Boris' 1984 papers, referred to earlier.

Palazzoli and Bruch described anorexia as being a particular psychosis, mid-way between the paranoid–schizoid and the depressive positions. This is now taken up by the concept of the pathological organisation (Steiner, 1993). I do not think all anorexics and anorexic bulimics are in the thrall of a pathological organisation, but some certainly are. Ellen West, (Binswanger, 1944) seems from her diaries and letters to have inhabited such a position, to the degree where her idealisation of death, aided and abetted by an internal gang (Rosenfeld, 1971) overran and overpowered her wish for life until she felt she had no option but to commit suicide.

For some anorexics there seem to be only two options: madness or death. Fenichel (1945) recognised that anorexia could be a defence against psychosis. Eglé Laufer implies that questioning a delusional belief system which operates around the body may lead to a psychotic breakdown.

> Any demand on the psyche for change of the body image ... can become a threat to the person's ability to relate to the external world in an undistorted form, resulting in a psychotic breakdown. (Laufer, 1991, p. 68)

> Eating disorder case histories frequently include Christian imagery of attaining the status of pure spirit by shedding the shackles of the body (e.g., Hogan, 1983; Wilson, 1983; Wooley and Wooley, 1985). An extraordinarily powerful wish for, and sense of, detachment from the physical realm contributes to the common delusion among severely anorexic individuals that radical weight loss will not bring death: The body will die, but not the core self. (Cross, 1993, p. 60)

Many anorexics feel superior and powerful because of their ability to deny their own needs, and so assume they are fundamentally different from other individuals. Omnipotence is about power and control and Palazzoli adds the effect of impact on the 'other' to the anorexic's fantasy of immortality.

> To begin with, she is prey to a most disastrous Cartesian dichotomy: *she believes that her mind transcends her body* and that it grants her unlimited power over her own behaviour and that of others. (Palazzoli, 1978, p. 223)

I shall look at this inability to know people as people in the next chapter, while not denying the validity of the above approaches. The above examples are taken from individual work with patients where the understanding comes out of the work itself. What I think may be a general trend is the tendency to focus on the narcissistic elements of the anorexic's or bulimic's behaviour. This, in turn, leads to a collusive focus between patient and therapist away from object relating as such. It is this lack which I wish to redress. In order to do this, I want to look at mother, her unconscious and its impact on her child.

Did I Have a Good Enough Childhood?

Babies do have to be cared for physically and emotionally. There is a reality of experience which these women have undergone and which is not given enough importance by Boris or Sohn. Mothering is not always good enough. Bruch stressed the real deprivations and deficits which the future anorexic suffered as a child. She led the way forward for the self psychologists such as Goodsitt (1983, 1985) and Swift and Letven (1984) who took her ideas about the failure of these children to recognise and interpret internal signals and external stimuli one step further. They saw over-stimulation as triggering off bulimic and anorexic episodes which prevented anxieties of an annihilatory nature coming to the fore.

This theme was also taken up by Krueger (1988) who saw the excessive overactivity of anorexics as a way of holding their physical and psychical selves together. Bruch saw this failure as belonging to the parents; the child had not been shown how to know, name or recognise her internal states. Bruch's work with these patients remained firmly in the conscious realm, but she was perhaps one of the first practitioners to recognise the terror beneath the facade of confidence and insouciance which many anorexics, in particular, present. These models have important implications for the technique of working with this group of patients – of the intricate attention which has to be given to the awareness and naming of patients' internal states – as far as this is possible. This recognition of the presence of powerful psychotic anxieties in eating disorder patients in general is vital, as is the recognition of the failure of effective parenting.

In the next chapter I wish to focus more on the mother's unconscious phantasies and conscious fantasies to show how they may impact on her daughter, using Winnicott's ideas of transitional objects and phenomena. They are connected.

A number of possibilities about the meanings of anorexia and bulimia have been proposed. Questions remain. What is it about the nature of the mother–child relationship that has meant separation is so hard? Is it, as has been suggested by Freud and others, a question of an unwillingness to compete with mother, to face the Oedipal situation in a straight-forward way? Is it to do with the presence of intense envy in the patient, which prevents separation from mother, for separation would mean having to experience the envy which in phantasy only leads to destruction?

Hilde Bruch's extensive experience with anorexic patients, and the awareness of the failure of ability to regulate affect are, I think, cornerstones to working with all groups of eating disordered patients. Her clinical experience is closest to my own, yet the annihilatory fears and presence of powerful destructive phantasies seem better fitted to a modern Kleinian technique where the deepest anxieties are interpreted and explored from moment to moment within the session. Both Bruch and her followers, I think, fail in practice to address the power of the negative forces and how they limit and indeed sometimes put these patients' lives at risk.

An alternative description would be to use the model of pathological narcissism, which seems only a small step removed from the idealisation of the death instinct and pathological organisations. Lorand (1943) noted the uncon-scious death wish fantasies of the mother towards the child and finally added that the whole problem centred around the fact that his patient had been unwanted. I want to take Bruch's work on the mother from the arena of the conscious into the unconscious. I hope that it is here that the missing piece of the puzzle may be found. If it is, it should expand our understanding of how psychotherapists work with these patients and give a wider canvas from which to draw individual understandings. I now want to turn to the mother, her pathology, and its possible effect on her foetus, her baby, her child and the eating disordered patient.

CHAPTER 3

The Body and Body Products as Transitional Objects and Phenomena

Eating disorders have never been simple. Symptoms are multi-determined and have multiple meanings. This has become increasingly clear over the last ten years. The earlier the difficulties start, the harder it is to find simple answers and solutions to any of the questions that may be asked. What can be said is that the complexity of eating disorders is ever more apparent, as is the pre-Oedipal nature of the disturbance. Anorexia and bulimia are no longer automatically seen as involving unresolved Oedipal issues. Problems can come from any stage of development (Schwartz, 1988). As the layers are peeled back so we delve deeper into primitive processes and the early mother–child relationship. 'The ultimate roots of bulimic behaviour reach into the earliest stages of life when the mental and the physiological aspects of experience are virtually inseparable' (Reiser, 1990, p. 246). I think it is useful to take things one step further back. It may seem hard to go back any further, but I think we need to return to the mother's body, the child in her womb and the conscious fantasies and unconscious phantasies she has had about her baby, both before and after she/he is born. This may provide additional ways of understanding the death wishes of these patients, their pathological narcissism and their failure to integrate body and mind.

One way to do this is to use Winnicott's (1953) concept of the transitional object to explain what the mother may be attempting to do for herself. It will then be possible to explore what this might mean for her child. I shall describe Winnicott's ideas of transitional objects in general terms before looking at more recent ideas on intermediate objects which will provide a means of exploring mother's pathology in a particular way. I shall then look at the historical apprecia- tion of the mother's presence in these disorders and how this can be understood. The effect that the mother's own frame of mind has on her baby, before, during and after his/her birth. The devastating impact on the child that may occur perhaps gives us a clue to understanding the difference between bulimics and anorexics and anorexic bulimics. A baby may be thought of as being a poor attempt by mother to create/use some kind of a transitional object. If this is the case then the effect on the baby of being used in this way needs to be explored. The components of the bulimic ritual can then be thought through and explored using this paradigm.

Winnicott's Transitional Objects

Winnicott's conceptualisation of the area of transitional space and transitional objects creates that much needed concept, one which can link and be a bridge between the inner and outer worlds, a place where the two interact unin- terrupted with the help of the first 'not-me' possession, as perceived by the infant, the third area of experience. The area described by Winnicott as being 'between the thumb and the teddy bear, between oral erotism and true object rela- tionship' (Winnicott, 1953, p. 89). Winnicott describes the special qualities with which the child embues its relation- ship with a transitional object:

(1) The infant assumes rights over the object, and we agree to this assumption. Nevertheless, some abrogation of omnipotence is a feature from the start.
(2) The object is affectionately cuddled as well as excitedly loved and mutilated.
(3) It must never change, unless changed by the infant.
(4) It must survive instinctual loving, and also hating, and, if it be a feature, pure aggression.

(5) Yet it must seem to the infant to give warmth, or to move,
     or to have texture, or to do something that seems to show
     it has vitality or reality of its own.
(6) It comes from without from our point of view, but not
     so from the point of view of the baby, neither does it
     come from within; it is not an hallucination.
(7) Its fate is to be gradually allowed to be decathected, so
     that in the course of years it becomes not so much
     forgotten as relegated to limbo. By this I mean that in
     health the transitional object does not 'go inside' nor
     does the feeling about it necessarily undergo repression.
     It is not forgotten and it is not mourned. It loses
     meaning, and this is because the transitional phenomena
     have become diffused, have become spread out over the
     whole intermediate territory between 'inner psychic
     reality' and 'the external world as perceived by two
     persons in common', that is to say, over the whole
     cultural field. (1953, p. 91)

Part of what I want to discover is if it is possible to understand
the earliest mother–baby dyad in terms of a narcissistic
mother's use of her baby to attempt to heal and find her own
way to a third area of experiencing. This is an unusual
approach to transitional objects. I am assuming that the
mother's development has gone awry and that she herself
has not progressed beyond the stage of confusion between
inner and outer. She is, in effect, attempting to use her
child's body improperly, as a transitional object for herself,
not as a transitional object proper, but as an intermediate
object as defined by Kestenberg (1970) and Kestenberg
and Weinstein (1988).
    They describe body products and food as being inter-
mediate objects. They are three dimensional, able to change
shape and fuse with the individual's body and separate from
it. They are attached and linked to the baby's body in a way
that transitional objects are not. From an observer's point
of view intermediate objects are not those given to others
by the child, but rather originate within the body itself.
They are linked to particular organs, such as vomit being
linked to the mouth and faeces to the anus, and are essential

bridges in the development of a secure body image. They are objects that are in themselves transitional to transitional objects. They are not fully transitional because of both their source and their function. For they are usually a bridge to mother herself. They change and decay and are destructible unlike true transitional objects. Intermediate objects may be thought of as being a special type of precursor to true transitional objects. They add an extra stage in the move from the body itself to the use of a blanket or teddy bear, a stage where, as yet, there is neither a secure internal mother, nor a secure internal body image. They change and decay quickly, unlike true transitional objects. They are usually a bridge to mother herself. The use of the child's body by the mother is what is at issue, and I shall start by looking at the perceived role of the mother in the literature on eating disorders.

Mother's Feelings about her Child

From the time of Gull (1873) onwards the problem of the eating disordered individual was seen, in part, as a problem of separation from mother. In one reported case Charcot disclaimed all responsibility for an anorexic's life when he discovered that his instructions to separate her from her mother had not been followed. His initial advice was then taken, and the mother left the daughter in the hospital where she did eventually recover (Charcot, 1889, pp. 210–11). The reasons why it was necessary to separate mother and daughter were not thought through, but the trend continued. Lorand tells of a patient who remembers her mother repeating to her many times: 'Mothers should never be born because they suffer so much' (Lorand, 1943, p. 302) and forty-one years later Lerner says of a patient: 'She related thinking about the many times her mother would tell her that she wishes she had not been born or that she was dead' (Lerner, 1983, p. 52).

As Schwartz says, 'It is this focus on the pathogenic role of the mother's unconscious psychic life that uniquely characterizes the psychoanalytic literature on the eating disorders' (Schwartz, 1988a, p. 33). It is what the early historical cases imply: despite the parent's conscious eagerness to help, there was something in the mother's relationship with her child which could threaten her life. It is not always unconscious, as Lerner's example shows. The father has not been forgotten, but his rare appearances in the material from now on mirror a trend among eating disorder families where the father is often a shadowy and absent figure (Neubauer, 1960; Yarrow, 1964). In practice this often means that the baby has to bear extra emotional burdens of which she is quite unaware.

Otto Sperling suggests that a mother perceives her child to be, in a very concrete sense, an extension of herself. This idea is well illustrated by David Krueger who quotes a mother saying to a therapist in a family therapy session: 'When she left home it was like losing a part of me – like my arm or part of my body' (Krueger, 1990, p. 262). Bird (1957) describes the failure of differentiation between the ego of mother and child and suggests that the child's ego 'responds directly to the id of the mother, with her ego reacting in turn to the id of the child' (Schwartz, 1988a, p. 35). This thought can perhaps be understood as an extrapolation of Melitta Sperling's (1949) idea that the baby is unconsciously viewed by the mother as representing a hated sibling or parent or a hated or a wished-for part of the self (particularly a phantasised penis).

> Moreover, for the first time she could remember what she had really been acutely aware of throughout early childhood, namely, that both her mother and father had been greatly disappointed that the patient, their last child, had not been born a boy. (Masserman, 1941, p. 334)

A mother's relationship to her child may be determined well before his/her birth.

> In working through the termination phase of her analysis she recognised that her pregnancies had not been in order to bear a live child, but in order concretely to assert her bodily separateness from her mother; the foetus inside her was concretely the hated mother controlling the body, who she expelled in phantasy through the abortions. (Pines, 1993, p. 132)

This woman's babies may be thought of as being an inter-mediate object, connected to the body zone of the vagina where the aim was to create a bridge to mother to attack her, but also to confirm her sense of separateness from her, to confirm her own body boundaries and body image.

This theoretical area is fraught with difficulties and there is much to be thought about. McDougall suggests that if a baby is a mother's sole source of libidinal and narcissistic satisfaction it will 'predispose the adult-to-be to the creation of what I have termed pathological transitional objects or "transitory objects"' (McDougall, 1989, p. 82). It is feasible that the baby might be seen as a fetish object and indeed Kestenberg and Weinstein say of intermediate objects: 'They are frequent forerunners of fetishes, whereby the object that stands for the maternal phallus has developed in analogy to the shape of the fecal column' (1988, p. 91). A baby cannot be thought to be an intermediate or transitional object in that it has its own life and neither does it change in the way either intermediate or transitional objects do. I would suggest that for some mothers, those whose own internal body image is insecure, their baby is used by them as though it were an intermediate or a transitional object. They do not know the difference.

Dinora Pines' example, quoted above, of a mother repeatedly having abortions, echoes a bulimic episode where the knowledge of the other is destroyed. Contrary to the Kleinian approach to the requirements for developing a secure inner world, there is no psychological intercourse, no internal creative couple who have given birth to the child. In phantasy, she is the sole provider of her own life and life with the object. She is also its destroyer. This phantasy is often present during the bulimic ritual:

> There will be time to murder and create,
> And time for all the works and days of hands
> That lift and drop a question on your plate. (Eliot, 1917, p. 14)

Mother can be eaten up, destroyed and created in phantasy during the bulimic ritual. It is a phantasy of self-creation, where no intercourse, no conception and no gestation is required.

> The vomiting symbol is a calling back by someone who is not able to tolerate separation and loss, which are experienced concretely, as though the act of swallowing the food 'disappears' the mother. (Shulman, 1991, p. 340)

By inference the vomiting brings her back. The lines between murder and creation are blurred, the lines between mother and child even more so.

> The foetus inside her own body now represents good and bad aspects of the self and of the object, and the mother may not give it a licence to live if she herself feels that she has never been granted one by her own mother. The pregnant mother's ambivalence towards her unborn child may reflect earlier intense ambivalent feelings towards her own mother, resulting in a difficulty in self-object differentiation and further difficulty in separation-indi-viduation ... Separation is unconsciously equated with death of the self or the object. Difficulties in accepting the mother as a good mother may lead to a woman's dif-ficulties in accepting the creative and life-giving aspects of herself. (Pines, 1993, p. 115)

The implication seems to be that the pathology of the mother may mean that she creates a world where her child has to remain attached to her, or in phantasy her very life is threatened.

> The effect of a pregnancy in such cases may depend on whether the fetus is experienced as a hostile, ego-alien invader (perhaps more often in restrictor cases), or as a comfortingly ever-present being more integral to the self and thus worthy of nurturance (perhaps more likely among bulimic patients). (Cross, 1993, p. 59)

The distinctions between the groups are not simple or clear cut, which is part of why work with these patients is so hard.

We are very far removed from a child's unconscious envy (above, pp. 24–7) and are closer to a state of mutual and perhaps terrifying confusion and entanglement of bodies and mind. How is the child likely to understand, take in and try to work with these experiences? All of these formulations support the idea of eating disorders being narcissistic in nature, but they go further in suggesting not only that the problem is one of separation of child from mother, but that it is the mother's pathology that is the issue. She is the heavyweight. The baby is but an extra in her mother's film.

> These patients have been attached to a domineering and controlling mother who attempts to attain passive submission and perfection for the child as her own fulfilment. Power and control exerted by the omnipotent mother is overwhelming, remarkably interfering with separation and individuation in all phases of the child's development. (Sours, 1974, p. 571)

Its possibly malevolent power is suggested by Rizzuto:

> The mother may impose from her own reality *something unrelated to the child, something that is not there*. She may attribute evil intent to the child's gestures or words or perceive them as excessive demands that must not be responded to. (Rizzuto, 1988, p. 374)

The state of the mother's inner world and her use of her baby may go some way to understanding why one individual develops bulimia, another both anorexia and bulimia and another bulimia by itself. It will only be a tentative thesis as the baby, its constitution and its experiences both with and without mother, together form the matrix of development. The pathology of a mother of an eating disordered individual can on occasion be strikingly similar to that of her child (Williams, 1994). It is implicit in the above example that the baby's function is to provide something for the mother, either as an object to attack, or use. How the baby is unconsciously perceived by the mother, whether she is allowed to exist in the mother's mind, and what kind of an existence she is allowed to have may influence the nature of the eating disorder the child develops. Anorexia and anorexic bulimia are both life threatening. Normal weight bulimia can be, but usually this is as a result of conscious suicidal impulses rather than the illness itself.

Anorexics' mothers are often described as being over-controlling and intrusive (Sperling, 1949; Bruch, 1973; Palazzoli, 1978, Wilson *et al.*, 1992); no separation by the baby is allowed. Many anorexics carry this feeling with them throughout their lives. They meet what they perceive to be their mother's needs and ambitions – usually intellectually and emotionally – and use their body as their own and their only arena of control and selfhood, which they can unconsciously and consciously use to attack and attempt to separate from mother. Normal weight bulimics have suffered intentional or unintentional neglect by their maternal caregiver, who is often a mixture of over-controlling and abandoning (Johnson and Conners, 1987; Johnson, 1991b). Their mothers are not, for whatever reasons, able to be constant in the care of their child. Anorexic bulimics' mothers have not been thought about in such general terms, but perhaps they manage to combine positions, showing extreme and violent ambivalence towards their children, being at one point over-controlling and overwhelming and at another abandoning and neglectful.

Baby as an Intermediate/Transitional Object

Rizzuto wrote: 'Food, feces, menstrual blood, the penis, and finally the fetus can all be experienced as the "other" within' (1988). I want to explore the idea of the mother trying to use her baby, both as an intermediate and transitional object. She wishes to use her baby both to confirm her own physical boundaries and as a bridge towards whole object relations. The use of the transitional object occurs in the area between the external and internal worlds. Winnicott makes it clear that the use of the object is what matters. It must be allowed to be loved, hated and attacked and it must also seem to have some vitality of its own, whether in texture, smell or movement. It is a stepping stone towards whole object relations and reality testing and its importance as a developmental move must be appreciated for its role to be understood.

All of this is meant to apply to babies and their bodies, not to adults – not to mothers and babies. Adults are meant to have progressed to art, literature and culture as their transitional phenomena (Winnicott, 1953). But a woman may have a baby in order to attempt to restore, create or get in touch with a good internal object, and to restore a missing element in her body image. This is when the trouble begins. Transitional objects can only be used effectively as tools towards whole object relationships if there is a good internalised mother to begin with. Winnicott puts it so: 'The transitional object may therefore stand for the "external" breast, but *indirectly*, through standing for an "internal" breast' (Winnicott, 1953, p. 94). Intermediate objects fill an in-between space before a stable internalised object and a stabilised internal body image is formed, and it is in this area that mothers can be thought of as trying to renegotiate with the help of their child.

The Child as an Essential Intermediate Object

A mother's peculiar relationship to the actual body of her baby is the focus of much psychoanalytic literature on eating disorders. That the mother is failing in a basic parenting task is very clear. Krueger explains this in terms of pathological narcissism:

> The preverbal experiences in the first year of life have failed to acknowledge and confirm a body self separate from the mother (Krueger and Schofield, 1987). It is as if the mother is incapable of accurate, consistent mirroring; of reflecting the child's aliveness, special distinctness, and body and psychic boundaries. In such cases the mother is unable to allow the child the opportunity for an autonomous, internally directed origin of experience and action. (1988, p. 58)

Cross makes the use of the body of the baby by the mother even more apparent:

> Among other factors, a parent's fetishistic focus on the infant's bodily functions and physical appearance – with

little interest in the infant's emotional states – or a parent's massively unempathic responses to the infant's bodily needs and somatic signals can foster the kind of early psyche/soma split that results in an eating disorder or delicate self-mutilation (Bruch, 1973; Doctors, 1979; Geist, 1985). (1993, p. 56)

Marie Maguire, in an article on bulimia and perversion, tells of a patient who perhaps was also used in an eroticised way by her mother.

There is a sense in which Mrs K sees her body as a pornographic object which she tries to control. From infancy, Mrs K seems to have experienced herself as a pretty, passive doll, to be displayed enticingly and played with by others. It has, she says, taken her a long time to realize that she can actively engage in, and feel herself a part of, her own sexual life. This sense of objectification is reflected in her concern with the physical functions of her body and its fluctuations of weight (1989, p. 120).

A patient of mine, a Ms P, suffered severely from bulimic anorexia. She was black, in her early twenties, and came to me after seeing many other professionals. She had attempted to take her own life on a number of occasions. She tried to destroy her body on a daily basis. She would drink a litre of wine per day, take sixty or so laxatives, eat little, or what she ate she would then vomit. She would walk into the room on legs which seemed to belong to a puppet. She looked and walked like 'Loopy Loo', a wooden puppet worked by strings. Her body came in, and she sometimes did. It was purely an appendage, a doll, in which she did not seem to have a presence. She had no use for it. She believed her body was indestructible, that death meant peace and contentment and still being alive. Her body could die. She would not. This psychotic belief rested on her knowledge that she was 'a thing'. She would often refer to her mother as having treated her like a doll or a toy. One day she brought in a photograph album for me to look at. In the pictures of her as a child, she was beautifully dressed and looked as though she had been placed, like a china ornament, on chairs, sofas or floors – to be taken out and dusted when the occasion merited it.

In our work together it became apparent that the only way she could behave towards herself was aggressively; this behaviour was both exciting and addictive. She was certain that she didn't want to change it. Over time, it became clear that she was unconsciously attacking an internal representation of her mother viciously and persistently, without ever being able to be aware of it. She wanted simultaneously to separate from her mother by murdering her own body. She had the delusion that she would then exist in her own right. At the same time her unconscious belief was that by killing herself she would also destroy her mother. This need to dispense with the self, and to use herself as she had experienced herself being used within her relationship with her mother, suggests how and why object relationships among these patients may appear warped and impervious to change. She behaved as though she were still her mother's intermediate object, if not her fetish, and by hurting herself she was thus hurting her mother and her mother's precious possession, herself. It was herself who was so inaccessible, as though she never had room to grow, except in response to mother's demands, demands that she internalised as her own.

The nature of the psychodynamics of the individual with bulimic or/and anorexic symptoms always necessitates a specific understanding, but this does not invalidate a general understanding of a symptom also being suggested. Not all anorexic bulimics perceive themselves as Ms P did, but I do think that the breadth of pathology needs to thought about in terms of the mother's unconscious and conscious use of her child, both physically and emotionally. I think what does distinguish these disorders from others is their narcissistic base, not only in the patient, but in the mother as well. Then detailed individual work needs to be done on the nature of her phantasies in relation to her damaged and narcissistic objects.

Effect on the Child

What is taken in by the child is the mother's own pathology. She is used by mother as an object, as a container (Lerner,

1983). But unlike a mother, a baby cannot process mother's feelings, whether good or bad, and unlike a transitional object cannot but be affected by them. The symptom of not eating, not digesting, can be seen as a clear message to mother that her child has either felt starved or that she needs to starve herself in order to free herself from mother. Mothers failure to contain and process her baby's emotions and her attempt to use her baby as a container for her own feelings means that the baby's emotions and experiences are not felt to have been recognised. This point is well described by David Krueger:

> These individuals' nuclear sense of self has not been cohesively formed, and remains disorganised and primitive. They have never integrated mind and body and are, therefore, unable to deny or defensively split them. The resulting maladaptive behaviors represent deficits rather than conflicts. The individual may not simply be denying a painful affect, she may have not developed an ability to recognise or distinguish different affects and bodily sensations. The narcissistic individual may not have a consolidated body image to either deny or achieve. (1988, p. 60)

This is not a good beginning.

> *Of the transitional object it can be said that it is a matter of agreement between us and the baby that we will never ask the question 'Did you conceive of this or was it presented to you from without?' The important point is that no decision on this point is expected. The question is not to be formulated.* (Winnicott, 1953, p. 95)

I think that many anorexics and bulimics are not asking this question from the inside out. The question is more fundamental for intermediate objects, because they come from inside rather than outside and their physical separateness from the body is therefore less in evidence. Anorexics are not able to question their belief that they are an object, and an essential one, for their mother. For to ask might threaten their mother's existence and their own. They do not know it can be asked, answered and survived. A patient of Charcot's was reported to have said: 'I prefer dying of hunger to becoming big as mamma' (Janet, 1929, p. 157). Mary, a clinical example in Sugarman and Kurash's article, 'The Body as a Transitional Object in Bulimia', says: 'I would rather *kill* myself than be like her, and that's when I throw up, when I become my mother' (Sugarman and Kurash, 1982, p. 65). An anorexic or bulimic anorexic is unlikely to be able to make use of transitional objects because a stable internalised representation of mother is so obviously absent.

An individual with an eating disorder cannot know how to move from intermediate to transitional objects – partly because she has been misused in a confused way, as both an intermediate and transitional object herself. She attempts to achieve an internal experience of mother by using herself as she felt used. It is in these terms that Sugarman and Kurash place their understanding of the use of a patient's body as a transitional object. However, the individual does not have a good internal representation of mother which would allow her to use transitional objects effectively. She only has the experience of being used as an intermediate object, and like her mother is busy trying to negotiate this earlier stage of development.

If the nursing experience has not allowed a good internal breast to be created, then a child will not be able to begin to make use of a transitional object, but is still able to make use of intermediate objects, which are used in a more direct form as a communication to others. The prototype for both of these comes from the nursing situation in the experience of the baby being held and playing. As Kestenberg and Weinstein have written, 'Both playing and holding, are the basic methods of building and maintaining the body-image' (1988, p. 82). They added:

> Secure holding provides the milieu for undisturbed drive satisfaction and the freedom to play. The feeling of mutual support facilitates the child's formation of a stable body-image, both of himself and of his nursing mother. This fosters the feeling of owning, of possessing both his own body and that of his mother. (pp. 86–7)

The play originates with the infant's own body – using toes and fingers – and the role of the transitional object is to be played with and held to recreate the illusion of being held safely by mother and able to play. The role of the intermediate object is to confirm the internal body image of the area connected to the product (faeces and anus for example) and bridge the gap from self to other by presenting the product to mother. Few eating disordered patients make it as far as using transitional objects. They remain fixed in the position of an intermediate object where the illusion of being safely held is exactly what is lacking and where a secure body image has not yet been achieved.

The absence of play is often very noticeable among this group of patients and the rigid structure of family life has often been observed, particularly among anorexic families. These patterns were noticed by Hilde Bruch in her pioneering work with anorexics and expanded upon by Philip Wilson in *Psycho-Dynamic Technique in the Treatment of the Eating Disorders* (1992). If the mothers of these patients had successfully negotiated the use of intermediate and transitional objects they would not have had to use their children in this way. In other words, I wish to suggest an area where intermediate objects were used by mother as though they were transitional but were not used effectively as stepping stones to whole object relations, because of the absence of a secure internal mother. This means that the patient has been played with by her mother, as though she were a transitional object, and she had to mould herself to her mother's wishes and expectations – in effect – to be without thought or the ability for self-directed action.

The Binge

This view of the absence, evacuation of thought, among some bulimics, is a point made by Diana Shulman in her article 'A Multitiered View of Bulimia', where she says:

> There is a sense of the bulimic ridding herself of her mind. She attempts to escape her capacity to think as thinking leads to painful thoughts about loneliness, loss, and

abandonment; she instead spends all her time evacuating her mind. The crowning achievement is a patient such as Ms Ames sitting in front of a blank television screen, which symbolises her mindlessness, or a patient, such as Ms Baker, who makes light of her weekend gorging and presents the details of her exploits almost as though they are concrete things subject to expulsion. (Shulman, 1991, p. 341)

What she does not address is how these psychotic islands, or perhaps autistic cysts (S. Klein, 1980) may be enabling. Shulman has suggested: 'Although the bulimic is able to return to the real world, she, too, is relying upon psychotic mechanisms during the periods of time when she is actively engaged in the binge–purge cycle' (1991, p. 342).

In my clinical experience her view is valid for some bulimics, some of the time, but a binge is not always a retreat into an autistic state, even for those for whom it may be so at times. A binge is multi-determined and may represent internal object relationships from any stage of development, and perhaps represents more than one at a time.

An adult with bulimic symptoms can be thought to be re-enacting her earliest and repeated experiences with mother during a binge (Krueger, 1988). A potentially and often momentarily nourishing experience becomes an unpleasant and destructive one. Mother is overwhelming and unsatis-factory and then has to be got rid of by vomiting. In the whole episode what is re-enacted is the experience of mother forcing herself and her wishes upon them, which are not nourishing and cannot be dealt with, except by vomiting them out, or not allowing them in at all, as is the case with anorexics. A fleeting experience of mother is found, but not consciously. The physical behaviour itself re-enacts being fed by mother. I now want to side-step the black hole of the bulimic episode itself, and look at its adjuncts: the vomit, the environment and the cleaning-up process.

Vomit as a Transitional Object

What are some of the possible meanings that food has once it has entered the mouth, food which is mixed with saliva and partially digested, whether in the form of vomit, in the mouth or outside the body, and in the form of the presence of large amounts of semi-digested food in the body itself? It is not the same as the food going in before it has been chewed, but the ingredients are usually recognisable. I shall also look at the presence of faeces, in and outside the body, and the nature of the procedures surrounding the ritualised ending of a binge. To elucidate the possible meanings I shall describe four clinical vignettes, focusing only on the progress of a binge and vomiting ritual. For Winnicott 'an essential feature of transitional phenomena and objects is a quality in our attitude when we observe them' (1971, p. 113). This is worth bearing in mind when reading about the patients cited below. David Krueger has written in this regard that:

> These individuals, because of their concrete, non-symbolic mode of operation, are not able to move to an external non-bodily transitional object. They seem instead to struggle to *create* a transitional object which *is* external, concrete and specific. The effectiveness of the object is fleeting, however, and can remain no more fixed in emotional consciousness than the defective internal images of body, self or other. (1988, pp. 61-2)

Krueger is using 'transitional' where I would use the word 'intermediate' due to its transitory nature, its creation within the body and its role in helping to define and restore a more complete internal body image.

Patient F

Patient F was a normal weight bulimic who binged and vomited many times a day. She did not feel able to work. After bingeing she would make herself sick. Sometimes the action would be very violent and the vomit would splatter back into her face, around the loo and onto her clothes and shoes. She would then spend time carefully cleaning up herself and the bathroom. She took numerous laxatives on a daily basis, and after the bowel movement or movements, she would change her clothes if necessary, and wash her body with care.

Patient E

E worked in an office and did not enjoy her job or her sur-roundings. She was extremely creative and used her skills to earn extra pocket money away from the office. While at work she would sit at her desk and whenever she could, she would eat a procession of biscuits, sandwiches and chocolate bars. She made them last all day long. She would eat something, and for an hour or two hours afterwards she would ruminate, bringing the food back up into her mouth where it would be chewed and swallowed again. This happened without her conscious awareness, although she could prevent it happening when she wanted or needed to.

Patient C

C was a very fit, normal weight bulimic. She lived at home with her mother and sisters. Her mother locked up the food at certain times during the day to try and stop her from bingeing. This failed, and C would binge secretly in her room. She kept the packaging and wrappers of the food she ate. When she had finished bingeing she would not go to the bathroom to be sick, as she was too frightened of being caught. She would vomit into plastic bags in her bedroom, which she then placed either in her wardrobe, her chest of drawers or under her bed. She did dispose of the vomit filled bags, but not at the first opportunity, which meant there was always more than one bag of vomit in her room.

Patient M

M was a normal weight bulimic who ate compulsively on a fairly regular basis. She worked in a hotel and did shift work. Sometimes she would binge and vomit, normally in the evening, before going to bed. After bingeing and vomiting she would then eat again, until she felt full, at which point she would lie down and go to sleep. She would be aware of the food inside her and her body shape on the bed as she was going to sleep. She would often report dream-like images before slipping into sleep.

Patients E, C and M use vomit in a rare and particular way. A normal weight or anorexic bulimic may have many different phantasies about her vomit, at different stages in her illness and on different days. For the nature of the vomiting and the vomit depends on what is eaten, what is drunk, how long it is allowed to stay in the stomach, and whether it is brought up by a clenching of the stomach muscles, or by using the hand or another object to tickle the back of the throat. Vomit can be thought about generally as being an intermediate object, as with Patient F. What is rare is its attempted use as a transitional object. For these patients have failed, as their mothers before them failed, to differentiate between intermediate and transitional objects. I think they turn to their body products, their intermediate objects, and try to turn them into transitional objects proper, in an attempt to integrate their body image and connect up with some experience of a good – rather than a controlling and abandoning – internal object.

I believe the above vignettes give credence to this idea. For patient E, the experience of partially digested food, which was chewed and swallowed, and chewed and swallowed again, worked as a method of assuaging her anxiety. The vomit was available, she played with it in her mouth, and this provided a third area of experiencing which removed her from an awareness of the barrenness of her inner and outer worlds. She could stay at work as a result. It proved itself to be enabling. It was for her a transitional object.

For patient C both her vomit and the remnants of food in the form of its wrappings and packaging were there for her to use as transitional objects, but for a limited time only. They were moved around the room, felt, played with, thrown away. In a bag, vomit has all the sensory requirements of a transitional object, a smell, a texture, a mobility and a life of its own. However, it is not a transitional object as it came from within her body and decayed quickly. It had to be thrown away after a certain time, as it became mouldy.

For a baby, going to sleep with a blanket in one hand is not unusual. So, too, for patient M, who could sleep once her transitional object of food was inside her. This is different from the sleepiness of the compulsive eater, for it was related to the vomit that had already been expelled, and hunger and destruction had been dealt with in fantasy. The good mother had been experienced and the bad mother had gone. Then came time for something to play with, to feel in a safe place with, which enabled her to sleep.

For patient F the clearing up process itself was soothing and provided an important in-between stage which enabled her to return to reality. The vomit may have helped to define and clarify her body boundaries, which in turn enabled her to take care of herself, however briefly. This use of the post-vomit time as a transitional arena is a common, though rarely talked about part of the bulimic ritual, for many normal weight and anorexic bulimics. Marilyn Lawrence does refer to it, although she understands it in a different way. She says: 'Some women spend hours cleaning up after themselves so that others will not discover the secret, messy part of them' (Lawrence, 1987, p. 199).

One of Winnicott's defining characteristics of the use of transitional objects is that there is no climax during play:

> It is to be noted that the phenomena that I am describing have no climax. This distinguishes them from phenomena that have instinctual backing, where the orgiastic element plays an essential part, and where satisfactions are closely linked with climax. (1971, p. 115)

I think this supports the thought of vomit being used as an intermediate object for bulimics, but not the act of vomiting itself. For there is a climax when at some stage the point is reached where the food has to be expelled. I do not think it is always orgiastic, although many would disagree, seeing the action of self-induced vomiting as being a symbolic representation of coitus, in one form or another (see Chapter Two). However, the very early nature of the disturbance suggests the act of expulsion of the food is a much earlier representation of a dynamic which occurred with mother and whose prototype may have been found in the feeding dyad.

Role of Stereotyped Rituals

Winnicott suggested that an addiction in adult life is an attempt to return to a time when the existence of transitional objects was not questioned. Yet he describes the third area as an area which is not challenged, because no claim is made on its behalf except that it shall exist as a resting place for the individual engaged in the perpetual human task of keeping inner and outer reality separate yet inter-related. (Winnicott, 1953, p. 90)

It is a place of illusion. It is this quality, more than any other that I think prevents the body from being understood as a transitional object during bingeing. For the whole point of the bulimic ritual is to work out what is 'me' from what is 'not-me' by the act of vomiting. This is the very opposite of the third area of experiencing where the question is never to be asked.

I do not, however, think there is ever only one way of under-standing an individual's bingeing behaviour. What bingeing means is always dependent on the underlying phantasies. Diana Shulman (1991) argues that a binge recreates the experience of mother without having to think about her. It deletes reality, and the thinking process is forfeited for a period of time. If this is accepted for even a few patients, it represents a concrete attempt to have a good mother inside. I think this can then help to explain the behaviour which takes place after the food has been brought up. It is here that the vomit in a small number of cases is used as though it were a transitional, rather than an intermediate, object. In a greater number of cases the vomit is used as an intermediate object to clarify body boundaries, and the cleaning-up ritual is used as though it were a transitional object. It is used to return to a world of whole object relating and perhaps provides the one area where a semblance of Winnicott's third area of experi-encing is appreciated, however painfully. It becomes a bridge back to reality. In work with patients, bingeing and vomiting are often used to enable them to undertake a task which they felt they could not do. For patient M bingeing and vomiting and then eating again allowed her to go to sleep; for patient E ruminating enabled her to stay and perform at work.

What I hope has become clear is the very varied and com-plicated nature of the internal worlds of these patients. This is demonstrated by their reliance on the bulimic ritual itself. A ritual that cannot be thought of as normal, or healthy, but is secretive and destructive. It must not be forgotten that viewing the bulimic ritual as being a way to create and use transitional objects is only one way of understanding it: a way which adds a more benign understanding to a ritual usually thought of as only being destructive. It seems likely that the less well the individual the more likely she is to try and use vomit as a transitional object. I would suggest that the same may apply to individuals who abuse laxatives excessively and in phantasy thus speed up and increase the production of faeces, with which they become overly preoccupied, in some cases becoming attached to the often painful and time-consuming process of evacuation and clearing up. Layers of meaning, from sexual phantasies to primitive destructive phantasies in relation to mother's and father's bodies, are always present and need to be explored. The one generalisation that seems to be possible is the narcissistic nature of these disorders, both in the patient and in her mother. Once that is said the range and nature of the disturbance needs to be looked at individual by individual.

The narcissistic quality suggests that many eating disordered patients' early experiences with their mother have prepared them for unreliable and misunderstanding relationships, where they survive by picking up on the expectations and wishes of the other and by responding to them, as far as they are able. They keep themselves in hiding. They are terrified of being known or seen and some indeed hardly know they have a self and believe that knowing it threatens their very existence (Rizzuto, 1988). For their mother may have used them as an intermediate object – which suggests that life apart from her would lead to decay and death.

This has important implications for the therapeutic relationship. The therapist, for instance, is likely to be experienced as mother, with her own hefty agenda. She is often thought of as being there for herself, the patient being there to help her, rather than vice-versa. There is rarely an awareness of a good object, but a definite awareness of a persecuting, controlling, envious bad one. Negative feelings tend to prevail, particularly with the more self-destructive patients, and the thought of a safe space will be alien. The make-up and intensity of these feelings will obviously be very different from individual to individual, but I think the idea of being aware of the importance of these patients' vicious perceptions of their internal relationship with their mother, and the expectations they bring to therapy, provides an essential space for the therapist. This is essential so that the therapist can think and show concern, and succeed in avoiding the powerful pull in the countertransference towards frustration, control and sadism in either tone of voice or content of interpretations.

By focusing on the mother's conscious or unconscious use of her baby as an intermediate object, I have tried to draw us up to the edges of Winnicott's third area of experiencing. I use 'up to' with care, as intermediate objects always remain precursors to transitional ones. Vomit, faeces and babies are all intermediate objects as they come from within, and cannot remain in an unchanged state. They either change or decay. Some bulimics and anorexic bulimics use vomit in such a way as to convince themselves that it possesses the characteristics of a transitional object proper, that it can be used as they like, for as long they like. It is this line of enquiry that I will pursue in connection with technique and the experience in both the transference and countertransference.

CHAPTER 4

Implications for Technique

The physical appearance of anorexic and anorexic bulimic patients is shocking. The outward appearance of normal weight bulimics is not shocking. This vital piece of information is usually ignored in the literature, where anorexics and bulimics are thrown together as though the experience of working with one is the same as working with the other, which, of course, it is not. Before looking in detail at some of the transference and countertransference issues presented by anorexics, anorexic bulimics and normal weight bulimics, I wish to look at why psychoanalytic work with these patients has often been opposed. Some have opposed it outright, and others have suggested that particular techniques are necessary to work with these patients. When I look more closely at working with eating disordered patients I hope some of the technical issues will emerge from the theoretical under-standings already referred to, and perhaps point to ways of thinking about material and making interpretations that allow these resistant patients to begin to appreciate that they have a digestive tract in their internal world which can be used to good effect.

As mentioned in the Preface, working with eating disordered patients can be frightening. On the surface and in reality, this is truer for anorexics and anorexic bulimics. They frequently put their lives at risk, and yet are often con-sciously unaware of it. To see a skeletal figure walking and talking is deeply disturbing. Skull's heads, death, torture, con-centration camps and starvation are some of the thoughts that instantly come to mind. Lasègue's frustration and feeling of impotence is apparent when he describes an anorexic's state of mind as being:

I might almost say a condition of contentment truly
pathological. Not only does she not sigh for recovery, but
she is not ill-pleased with her condition, notwithstand-
ing all the unpleasantness it is attended with. In comparing
this satisfied assurance to the obstinacy of the insane, I
do not think I am going too far ... 'I do not suffer, and
must then be well,' is the monotonous formula which has
replaced the preceding, 'I cannot eat because I suffer'.
(Lasègue, 1873, p. 151)

Extremely primitive feelings are stirred up by anorexics and
anorexic bulimics, feelings of resentment, anger, hate and
rage. That a fellow human being should so damage herself
and not want to be fed or recover is almost unbearable. Many
people wish to feed them up before they will work with
them. They do not believe it is possible for individuals to
make sense, or perhaps be made sense of, at such a low weight.
I think this is the reason why Bruch (1970, 1973, 1978),
Palazzoli (1978), Garner and Garfinkel (1982) and Hsu
(1986) suggest that analytic work should not be undertaken
until a certain amount of weight has been regained. Their
rationale is that thought is not possible below a certain
weight. Thought is a problem for many anorexics and
bulimics, but it is not one that is affected by weight. Concrete
thinking and difficulties in symbolising are among the basic
features of eating problems, regardless of the particular
theoretical stance that is adopted (Boris, 1984a, 1984b,
1988; Sohn, 1985; Shulman, 1991). Eating and digestion
can be thought of as being metaphors for taking in experiences in the world and effectively processing them – or not.
Unconscious phantasies are rife regardless of weight and are
open to interpretation. In *Psycho-Dynamic Technique in the
Treatment of the Eating Disorders* (1992), Wilson *et al.* give
examples of working analytically with patients who weigh
half their average weight.
    Bruch (1962, 1965, 1970, 1978), Crisp (1965, 1967,
1968, 1980), Dally (1969) and Palazzoli (1978) went even
further and argued that working psychoanalytically with
these patients should be avoided. Professor Arthur Crisp and
Dr Peter Dally are psychiatrists, not psychotherapists, and

their bias may come from personal and professional beliefs about psychotherapy in general, rather than the specific phenomena of eating disorders. Bruch is a special case and changed her mind over the years, as psychoanalytic technique itself became more flexible. She was opposed to strictly classical technique because of its failure to contain these patients adequately, for whom silence is often not tolerable. Palazzoli seconded Bruch's approach to working in an educational rather than analytic way with anorexics. She found the difficulties of working psychoanalytically on an individual basis with eating disordered patients was so great, and the rate of improvement was so slow, that she moved rather suddenly from individual to family therapy.

The Problem

The main problem in working with these patients is that the very process of taking things in has gone wrong, as has the process of mental digestion. These are other words to describe very early confusion in the mother–daughter relationship. There is very little room for manoeuvre. Using such basic and primitive terms tends to steer me towards a Kleinian understanding of projective identification – not normal projective identification but virulent projective identification – the type which Enid Balint felt had taken place within some of her patients, whom she describes in her paper 'On Being Empty of Oneself' (1993, pp. 37–55). Bion's (1962) paradigm of container and contained also comes to mind.

The absence of a container and the function of containing can be thought to have been present in both the patient and the mother. This leads to a very difficult place, one I have tried to think about and elucidate by using Winnicott's (1953) idea of transitional objects and Kestenberg and Weinstein's (1988) idea of intermediate objects to exaggerate the absence of an experience of the self, apart from being simultaneously a leaky and chaotic container for, and an extension of, mother. The patient's needs or wants may only be met by accident or in secret in order to preserve the fantasy of not having a separate life in either mother's or her own eyes. I want to use the idea of the baby as an intermediate object as a metaphorical way to understand some of the pressures which the therapist experiences in the transference. In so doing, I hope to allow the therapist the freedom not to behave in a neglectful or sadistic fashion in the therapeutic encouter.

It seems to be necessary to introduce real objects, not just internal ones, into the picture. A Kleinian understanding does much for narcissism and understanding the confusions of the divide between self and other but does little for the necessary impact of separateness in reality. Anorexic and bulimic symptoms can be thought about as being ways to separate, to attempt to distinguish 'me' from 'not-me', both internally and externally. But a Kleinian approach only deals with one half of the problem. It addresses the concrete nature of the symptoms, the part-object relations and the thoughts and underlying phantasies. The differences between Klein and Winnicott revolve around their respective understanding of the internal and external worlds and the role of internal versus external objects. Kleinians believe that there is a very definite distinction between inner and outer worlds with the action taking place in the internal world. In my opinion the line between external and internal is almost non-existent, rather than definite, as the sense is that it is only the internal world and internal objects that matter. Winnicottians not only recognise the external world but believe it does impact on an individual's internal object relationships. This is why Winnicott could conceive of an in-between 'space', and even in-between 'objects': his ideas of transitional space and transitional objects. For Kleinians this is not a possibility, as the internal objects are so primitive and so embedded in the unconscious that for an external object to represent both an internal and external object would suggest ill health, rather than a developmental stage, as Winnicott believes.

Winnicott's viewpoint suggests that the interplay between inner and outer, between external and internal worlds, happens somewhere, in a zone, a space, in the external world, which is experienced as being neither internal nor external. For Kleinians there is no zone between the internal and external worlds. For bulimic patients it is this very zone between inner and outer which they are trying to clarify and define in a very concrete way, with the assistance of the bulimic symptom. The confusion for both the anorexic and the bulimic is the tremendous impact that the external world, in the form of food (representing input, stimulation of any kind), has on their bodies. The internal and external world do impact upon each other, and there is arguably a third area between them, and it is here that Winnicott's ideas are useful, for they provide a space, an in-between, that is so clearly lacking for anorexics and bulimics.

This is the problem for the therapist. The patient, whether anorexic or bulimic or a mixture of the two, will have spent her life ensuring that she is not known, at the same time as longing to be known and be given the room to grow. Ana-Maria Rizzuto describes it thus:

> The patient's most persistent defence is an ever-present attempt to control the analyst. The motive for the defence seems to be to prevent the analyst from making emotional contact with the patient. In fact, if such contact is not introduced very gradually it evokes massive anxiety. (1988, pp. 371–2)

She goes on to explain how the mismatch may have come about:

> It stands to reason that the wish to speak in order to communicate affect and inner experience requires, as an indispensable condition, repeated experiences of achieved bodily communication during the first year and of verbal communication during the second and third years. External safety, however, is not enough. Self and object representations – the internal world – must also offer a modicum of safety for affects to be put into words. Without this safety the attempt at describing feelings may bring about massive anxiety or a discharge in action (Green, 1977, p. 150), as happened with Wilson's patient who had to vomit his words. (1988, p. 383)

Being cumulatively misunderstood is traumatic, and the difficulty with working with these patients is trying to provide a safe space in which understanding can be sought and found. Within the transference the likelihood is of being expected to be a brutalising and misunderstanding mother, who is only there to use her 'child' or 'patient' for her own needs and who cannot understand, contain or process any of the patient's material. In the transference this is what they wish to elicit from their therapist, and they often succeed. Methods vary, from silence to rushing streams of material to material so confused or encoded that comprehension often feels impossible. The patient has adapted to not being understood or known, by withdrawing and becoming apparently un-understandable. Other people are there to be provoked so that the patient may be moved into action, reaction or puppet-like activity – all in order to protect a self which is often nascent in form and substance and which is hidden. To be good is to be safe, to do as the therapist wants, for to act as a near-perfect intermediate object ensures the absence of attack, and may even hold out the possibility of good feedback. This often makes psychoanalytic psychotherapy very hard for these patients. All experiences which set off an awareness of difference in mother or self must be avoided. Experiences may be good, bad or indifferent, but they are to remain hidden. For some patients, sustenance of some kind seems to be drawn by retreating temporarily to a near autistic state during bingeing (Shulman, 1991).

Getting Around the Problem

This is how the eating disordered patient has managed to survive, and it this very dilemma which Bruch (1973, 1978), Palazzoli (1978) and others have tried to circumvent by avoiding working in a classical psychoanalytic way with these patients. The difficulties may seem insurmountable. As Tedesco and Reisen comment on Mark J. Gehrie's work with patients:

None of his cases of eating disorders were in analysis in the strict sense because none could psychologically survive in the atmosphere of abstinence characterized by a classical analytic procedure (1) emergence of intense anxiety followed by active flight from the process, or temporarily, from the treatment itself; (2) a non comprehending blankness and sense of isolation. In no sense was there an introspective capacity to allow for the development of a therapeutic alliance. (1985, p. 156)

This is very similar to the experience of working with these patients which Hilde Bruch describes in her book *The Golden Cage: The Enigma of Anorexia Nervosa* (1978). What is implied (and is voiced by Lasègue) is how difficult it is for the therapist to tolerate the anxiety, frustration and the wish to cure these patients – to react – to become the 'user' of the patient, to calm oneself, rather than trying to understand, tolerate and interpret their distress. These countertransference dilemmas are well expressed by K. J. Zerbe in an article entitled, 'Eating Disorders in the 1990s: Clinical Challenges and Treatment Implications':

Countertransference dilemmas can be tempered by recognizing the principal relationship struggles in the treatment process: (1) the patient's deep masochistic trends, which contend with omnipotent wishes to control the therapist or to render the therapist the 'bad object' (Lerner, 1991; Novick and Novick, 1991); (2) the patient's tendency to identify with the aggressor (A. Freud, 1936; Ganzarain and Buchele, 1988); and (3) the therapist's excessive need to change the patient, particularly vis-a-vis the eating behaviour (Boris, 1984a; Gabbard, 1990). (Zerbe, 1992, p. 180)

My own uncertainty about Bruch's educational approach is that it fulfils the conditions noted above, and places the therapist in the position of being a source of all knowledge and perhaps unconsciously recreates an experience of a mother who wishes, in the child's experience, to control her child like an object, as an extension of herself. This is not to disregard the fact that the patient may be simultaneously being understood for the first time. Fact feeding does not allow the patient to find her own solutions and bypasses the muddle, which is an essential component on the search for some recognisable and nameable internal experience. Bruch entirely ignores the unconscious elements of the conflict between mother and child. Palazzoli supports Bruch's approach, particularly its existential aspects in relation to an exploration of the here and now and being-in-the-world. She suggests intensive psychotherapy with the involvement of the parents is necessary. From a technical point of view, she thinks the couch is too frightening to be used initially with these patients, that they must be told that food is the symptom not the problem and that 'References to the transference situation are best avoided, not least because the patient finds them too painful' (Palazzoli, 1978, p. 128). She says later: 'In my view the sexual fears of anorexic subjects are, in fact, almost invariably the expression of their fear of psychological "invasion"' (p. 157). She says of bulimic anorexics,

> In particular I found that patients suffering from severe bulimic crises displayed thought and communication disorders not present in patients who keep strictly to their reduced diets. Family observations also seem to suggest that major bouts of bulimia go hand in hand with psychotic confusion, violence and a complete breakdown of family communication. (p. 205)

There is a tone of despair, defeat and violence in her descriptions, yet the problem she describes is the same one throughout: how to make contact with these individuals without triggering off massive anxiety, flight or fight mechanisms and/or annihilatory terrors. As I have said, Palazzoli finally abandoned individual work in favour of family work. The strands of Bruch's ideas concerning compliancy and deficit in the child were taken up and elaborated by the self psychologists who saw the analyst as acting as a necessary self-object who performed a missing function for the patient, which she would eventually manage to take up for herself. This variation on the theme of narcissism is an important one, but what self psychologists avoid are the complicated interactions which take place in the inner world, particularly the depth and complexity of the patients negative feelings. For instance, they only recognise anger as a realistic response to a narcissistic wound (Kohut, 1971), which means their self-object representations will tend to focus on what is lacking, somewhat at the cost of working with very primitive and destructive phantasies.

Envy has no place at all. The primitive oral, anal and urethral sadism of Klein is nowhere to be found. It is this very sadism which has to be thought about and experienced and not acted out in the countertransference, which is the crucial element in working successfully with these patients. The intensity of the feelings of violence obviously varies from patient to patient, but what matters is the awareness from the start of treatment that the therapist is unconsciously going to be persuaded to be or feel sadistic or to use an attacking tone of voice. The aim of the patient is to be invaded, to feel controlling and so controlled, so that no separation is known or experienced. There is in effect no space to play or think. This is a point made indirectly by Cross in her article on eating disorders and delicate self-mutilation:

> Internal and external sadomasochism are linked through the common element of the body; other people are manipulated as if they were extensions of the body, and functions or parts of the body are tyrannised as if they were unruly persons. (Cross, 1993, p. 62)

Klein's emphasis on primitive sadistic unconscious phantasy sheds light on much of the material which anorexics and bulimics bring to the consulting room. So too do Winnicott's ideas on transitional space and objects. Theoretically, as described above, the two are not compatible. It may be that both positions are needed and that the effect of the lens of the internal world is variable, dependent not only on its own ever-fluctuating construction but on the intensity and nature of the light of the external world.

The ego psychologists' scientistic approach makes things appear more cut and dried and less bewildering and confused than I have found them to be in practice. Their 'by the numbers' approach is troubling and their language somewhat alien. Their belief that a conflict-free sphere of the ego can

be facilitated in themselves and their patients makes working
sound easy, with the consequence that the question of who
is who from moment to moment in the session is just not
explored. Philip Wilson suggests that while dyadic material
is being worked with, the patient should be seen face to face,
and when Oedipal material appears a move to the couch
should be made. He says,

> Whilst some cases can be analysed with classical technique,
> in most patients the initial technique involves focusing
> on dyadic material. Patients are seen face to face with early
> interpretation of manifestations of their impulse disorder.
> Only when there has been a modification of the archaic
> superego with ego maturation and a shift from part-
> object relationships can triadic oedipal material be
> interpreted. Recently developed techniques that enable
> therapists to interpret and resolve severe regressions
> (primitive mental states) were presented. These include
> new research on oral-phase dream symbols, such as sand
> and stone, xerostomia, and projective identification.
> (Wilson, 1992, p. 71)

Having stated that the methods put forward by the ego psychologists are often alienating, I do agree with Philip Wilson's
appreciation of how early and powerful the transference can
be with these patients. He says, 'The process that many
analysts seem not to have understood is that a most intense
pregenital transference has already developed at the start of
the analysis' (Wilson, 1992a, p. 39). Wilson is very aware
of the transference and the countertransference, but he uses
the latter as a guide for what *not* to do, rather than as a
powerful instrument of communication between patient
and therapist:

> The analyst has to distinguish carefully between counter-
> actions and countertransferences in the analysis of these
> patients. The analyst experiences all the conscious
> reactions to the patient's provocative behaviour and
> acting in and acting out that one experiences with a
> rebellious child, except that the eating disordered patient
> is not a child and is far more provocative, deceptive and

manipulative (Wilson 1986, 1987; Wilson *et al.*, 1985). (Wilson, 1992a, p. 55)

I would go further and say that it is *only* by being closely attuned to the transference and countertransference dynamic – and by containing and interpreting the latter – that effective work with these patients can take place. This shift from being wary of countertransference to making use of it can be seen as one of the most striking developments in modern Kleinian thought (Brenman Pick, 1985; Young, 1994).

Countertransference Problems

The somewhat denigratory nature of the words used by Wilson to describe the provocative behaviour of these patients is the norm. It was not only Palazzoli (1978) who gave up working in an individual way with these patients. They do stir up powerful and primitive feelings in their therapists, as can be seen in some of the literature. Leslie Sohn (1985) suggests bulimic patients evoke anorexic feelings in their therapists, and that anorexic patients evoke bulimic feelings in their therapists. In my experience the split between the groups is not so clear cut, with both groups illiciting anorexic and bulimic feelings in the therapist. What is of even greater interest is his frustration at the inaccessibility of these patients that can be glimpsed in his writing:

> This was borne out in the analytic work, where not only was there neglect in general of the analytic food, but a repetitive nagging demand that each, or parts at least, of each interpretation should be differently couched. This was usually accompanied by interruption into most interpretations. If she started to enjoy an interpretation she would make herself unaware of her enjoyment and therefore unaware of an analyst; if however the interpretation was not enjoyed she was obsessed by the interpretations that were to come. (Sohn, 1985, p. 51)

A little later, he offered the opinion that:

> The anorexic continues her appetiteless behaviour while greedily demanding an impossible series of satisfactions;

> the bulimic patient stays greedily searching for unenjoy-
> able satisfactions from an object, while remaining without
> appetite, understanding and awareness of her state. (p. 55)

According to Sohn what happens is that the therapist ends
up with a metaphorical eating disorder; he or she feels her
therapeutic food cannot be eaten or cannot be tasted, or will
never be enough. This then leaves the therapist feeling
frustrated and short of options. In this situation it seems to
me that the patient is not being helped to become her own
therapist. Philip Wilson also talks despairingly of working
with bulimic anorexics: 'The analyst is derided and rejected,
as are his/her efforts to know the patient's private thoughts
and feeling' (Wilson *et al.*, 1992, p. 370). Earlier, Wilson
suggested that:

> The bulimarexic seems to be making every attempt to
> render the analyst impotent as a person and as her helper.
> Every avenue the analyst tries seems to find the patient
> ready to block access. No matter what the analyst does,
> the patient appears ready to pick a fight. (1983, p. 190)

Furthermore, he opined: 'In the countertransference the
analyst experiences exhaustion, discouragement, anger,
humiliation, and a wish to get rid of the patient' (Wilson *et
al.*, 1992, p. 372).

Before working out how to get through to these patients
and how to connect to them it is important to know from
what they are protecting themselves and their therapists.
These experiences of despair, frustration and fury have to
somehow be thought about and used to help patients within
the therapeutic relationship. By thinking once more about
mother's unconscious feelings towards her child and her
possible use of her as an intermediate object I think some
of the intensity of the experience can begin to be thought
about. For these patients, being known is dangerous. Before
addressing this I wish to explore how patients receive interpretations from their therapists.

The Patient's Point of View

They dread the power of the analyst's words to invade them as a destructive weapon, to manipulate them or harm them internally. One of my patients used to warn me not to name her emotions, or to make any statement about her because she would feel invaded by me. (Rizzuto, 1988, p. 370)

She also makes the point that the patient feels herself to be an object in her own eyes and in her mother's. This is experienced by Marie Maguire in an extremely concrete way in the transference and countertransference:

However, because in childhood, there was, in reality, no other involved adult who could help her to separate psychologically, in the early stages of her therapy Mrs K. remained preoccupied with an unusually intense physical identification with her mother's body. She experienced herself and her mother as identical, both simultaneously beautiful and repulsively fleshy. In her therapy sessions, over a period of time, it was as if, in fantasy, she wrapped herself around me and became me. When this first happened, I had the sudden alarming feeling that, without understanding how or why, the ground had been cut from under my feet and I had lost all sense of who I was. When I expressed this feeling of intense disorientation, Mrs K. then began to voice her fantasy of having stepped into my skin, sat in my chair and become the therapist rather than the patient. At this point, I began to regain my capacity to think and understand. During these sessions Mrs K. arrived wearing clothes as similar to mine as possible. For the first time in her therapy, she became visibly enraged. Her anger focused around the fact that I wore an unpredictable colour, one she disliked too much to copy. If she could actually experience herself as being me or her mother, rather than a separate individual in her own right, then in fantasy she could control us. Imagining that she possessed all our attributes, she need not feel her usual sense of inequality and envy in relation to us. (1989, p. 119)

Marie Maguire was able to use her experience in the counter-transference to enable her to understand the process that was taking place. So the problem at least becomes a little clearer. It is how to make a link, a link which is thinkable about in words, rather than simply being experienced as a takeover bid or an attack from either therapist or patient or both. This can be thought of as being part of a very early scenario where mother saw child as an extension, a part of her self, and the only way to grow was to become mother, separation and separateness were untenable. The route to finding the self was unknown. What is needed with these patients is compassion; injections of frustration are their bread and butter. They do not expect or hope to be understood.

This difficulty regarding making and reflecting on links is well illustrated by a normal weight bulimic patient of mine. She was very concerned with trying to think about her sexuality, her body and about reproduction. She felt handicapped by the very concrete nature of her thought. She was unable to imagine a link being formed, and found the end of sessions particularly painful, when she felt forced to leave when she wanted to stay. Links were not allowed or acknowledged if they were outside of herself. Here are two examples from her material which help to illustrate this point.

The first example is of her telling me with some difficulty about drinking three pints of water before the session and at the end of session going to the bathroom and peeing it away. Although it was hard for her to tell me (that she did so was unexpected), she saw it as paralleling what went on in our sessions. During the sessions a whole lot of 'bad stuff' (her words to describe strong emotions) was stirred up. By peeing at the end of the session she felt she had got rid of the feelings. She felt cleansed and very good at the end of the session. This was so. It was also true that it was a way of her controlling the content of the session. She could have it inside and get rid of it at the end of the session. I was, metaphorically, peed away until the next time, when she could magically recreate me inside herself before the session and then do with me as she wished. The action took place inside her, and she felt responsible for it.

What was different was her practising the experience of having a space inside, one that she could use in a non-destructive way and that she was letting me know about it, and witness it. She was practising in the only way she knew, a concrete way of being full and empty, but one which was not actually or potentially physically damaging. The idea of having any kind of a feminine internal space was a very new experience for her, and babies were in her mind still products of eating, drinking or defecating. There was apparently no phantasy of a copulating couple, the phantasy was rather of self-fertilisation. In phantasy the wish was to be able to fertilise herself and give birth, without having to know of her own birth, the fact of her parent's intercourse and her dependent relationship to them.

A dream from a couple of weeks later again shows the hope that magical thinking can bypass the painful, step-by-step process of growth. In the dream she spoke of a four-year-old girl who was listening to her father giving a speech from a podium. The child then went up to the podium and continued the speech. People commented on how precocious she was. In one move she went from being a four-year-old girl to being a father, with a father's abilities and accomplishments. In the dream she takes his place; he is no more. Not only has a change of sexual identification occurred, but all of the in-between stages are missing. In real life her father had left abruptly, and she did indeed feel as though she had taken his place in relation to her mother. She has spent her life behaving like a grown man while feeling like a four-year-old girl. The deal she struck with her mother, her internal mother, was that mother would give her some love if she played the role of a man. If she competed with mother, not only would she have to forfeit her love, and risk being attacked by her, she would have to come to terms with the agonising loss of her father and thus have to face her unresolved pre-Oedipal relationship with her mother.

Redefining the Problem

Ana-Maria Rizzuto, in her article 'Transference, Language and Affect in the Treatment of Bulimarexia' (1988), provides a way of thinking about anorexic bulimics and by inference normal weight bulimics and anorexics, in terms of what is to be known and what is not. Hidden meanings and secrets are waiting to be found out, and often seem to be just out of the reach of eye or hand. Rizzuto suggests that the defence against the transference is the transference itself. Mother and child have colluded to avoid understanding the subjective experience of the child. In the transference there is no wish to talk, as there is no belief in being understood or heard. There is a wish to avoid the repetition of the trauma of not being understood, or of actively feeling attacked. Words, as a form of self soothing, are not available to them. They are felt to be overwhelming stimuli, the affects of which cannot be experienced, for there is no safety in which to experience them. To repeat what I said earlier, the patient feels herself to be an object in her own eyes and in the eyes of her mother.

I think the use of the word 'collusion' gives an unfair intentionality to the child's behaviour. Certainly as adults, eating disordered patients often present through a series of smoke screens, misunderstanding mirrors, which have to be seen through and thought about in detail before sense can be made of them. It is not so much that as children they colluded with their mother, rather that their signals were misunderstood, in different ways, and this misunderstanding was taken in, along with mother's feelings and wishes, until the only safe way of trying to get things from mother was to steal. Mary Magdalen stretched out a hand to touch Jesus without being seen – hoping to gain strength by doing so. Anorexics and bulimics often feel the only way to have something from mother which does not diminish her or attack themselves is by theft. They pray they can feed without it being known or experienced by mother. At the same time stolen food is tainted, and although it can be eaten, it is difficult for it to be nourishing, as in phantasy it has to be self-created and not part of an object relationship. For if it is recognised as having been stolen from mother, retribution is awaited. So it cannot be allowed to lead to growth.

The Location of Interpretations

The area of action or interaction which is possible with these patients is very hard to find. The ground needs to be prepared before interpretations can be used or thought about. In his classic paper on 'The Observation of Infants in a Set Situation' (1941) Winnicott has described a scenario that I think offers an analogy as to how interpretations could be offered to eating disordered patients. The situation in his paper is a contrived one, where a mother and her baby (who is within a specific age range) come together into Winnicott's consulting room. He has placed on his desk a spatula, and the observation involves watching how the child responds to the spatula on the desk. The differing approaches, the types of play, or the lack of them, all provided extremely useful information about the nature of the child's relationships and inner world.

I think this is how interpretations need to be given to anorexic and bulimic patients. They have to be offered. They must not be thrust down the throat of a patient. The timing and the tone has to be considered and close attention has to be paid to how the interpretation/spatula is handled, chewed and possibly discarded. Patient M, to whom I have already referred, used to swallow my interpretations whole. It took some time before I became aware of what had happened. She would talk about herself in a way which was strikingly familiar, and I realised that my words and phrases had been directly and unconsciously purloined by her. They would appear months after I had said them, just as I had said them, whole and undigested, as though they were her own. If I had failed to notice this process, which it would have been easy to do, I could not have appreciated the relevance of the appearance of what I had said in some sort of a digested form.

A space has to be found where some reflection is possible for both patient and therapist. In practice this is extremely hard, particularly with long-term anorexic and bulimic anorexic patients and can only come about once very powerful feelings have been experienced and survived in the transference. This is not to state that things then become easier but there are at least moments of possibility. Deidre Barret and Harold Fine suggest that patients cannot tolerate penetrating interpretations:

> Interpretation, when initiated by the therapist, never really worked because it was construed as being commanding and could set up resistant behaviour. Liz remained essentially sombre, but began to be able to tolerate gentle humour. (1990, p. 266)

Harold Boris makes the point with which I agree – that interpretations have to be presented in the transitional space:

> The anorectic problem is the boundlessness of her desire on the one side and the envy on the other and the dizzying simultaneity of the two ... Both combine to hate and mentally obliterate the separateness and distinctness of the object. There is no transitional space – the not-me, but yet not-other space – that transitional objects require. The anorectic lives, as it were, without a skin. Others, in their incandescent desirability, impact on her with detonating force. And this is the problem ... The analyst, then, needs to work in a transitional space. He cannot work on or in his patient. (1984b, p. 437)

The paradox is that this is what these patients lack and what I think Barret and Fine are recognising when they say direct interpretations were not tolerable to their patient. However, humour can be, and I think the tone of voice can also be, a powerful tool against the anticipated destructiveness of the internal mother, whom they have tried to provoke in the transference. Alan Sugarman, analysing a bulimic, has noted:

> Her wishes to be regarded so highly made it difficult to find ways of phrasing interventions that would not feel critical. To focus on a 'problem' felt to her like an attack on not being perfect. (1991, p.17)

Silent Interpretations: Toleration of Countertransference Feelings

Interpretations can only be made effectively once some kind of safe arena has been created. The analytic frame itself provides some safety, as does the non-attacking position of the therapist, which is often very difficult to maintain, for there is much pressure from the patient to react in a hostile way, to ensure a repetition of a violent and intrusive object relationship, where there is no space between. The space has to be filled or awareness of separation is unavoidable. I think the first step is the toleration of powerful countertransference feelings which come from an extremely primitive layer of the child–mother relationship. According to Zerbe,

> As Gabbard (1989) has suggested in a different context, such silent processing is often quite helpful in diagnosing the patient's internal object relations and in modifying projections for reintrojection. Such 'silent respect for the patient's central self may be the only viable technical approach to fostering the therapeutic alliance' (Gabbard, 1989, p. 533) because it provides the patient with the time and empathic understanding to establish autonomy. Only then can the eating disorder be controlled, because the patient desires change for the self and not for the therapist. (1992, pp. 179–80)

This point of silent and compassionate toleration of what is nearer to chaos rather than muddle is also stressed by Boris (1984b) as being instrumental in providing the patient with an opportunity to emerge from her silent, secret shell. It is what I think of as the toleration of vomit within the sessions – undigested material which patients need to bring up again and again before they can begin to use it as an intermediate object and then as a transitional object with the help of the therapist in the transference:

> But in the end, it is the analyst's own quiet tolerance of the muddle and uncertainty, of the gradualness of approximations, of error and apology that makes it possible for his patient to simply come to be. In being resides the experience that when genuinely experienced leads to the insights with which development is facilitated. The capacity for both parties to the analysis to manage the presence of the absence of certainty is what, more I think

than anything, to be or not be the conducive factor. (Boris, 1984b, p. 441)

The therapist has to become what the child felt the mother could never be, a container and processor of her feelings, thoughts and terrifying anxieties. The expectation is to receive them back in an amplified and frightening form, and this is what the therapist has to try to avoid. The patient expects to be force fed or starved and to do the same to the therapist. The vomit has to be accepted as worthwhile material, however incoherent, disconnected and fractured it may seem. At some stage the time comes when it is possible to use countertransference feelings to make sense of the material and to allow an interpretation to be given some form of a hearing, however briefly. I want to give a fairly long clinical example to illustrate this point. It is a session with patient M which took place some four weeks before the Christmas break and which I want to use to illustrate the complex nature of the interaction between patient and therapist. I will try to decode the session to illustrate the point about transitional space, the pressures in the transference and the very sparse connections that could be made.

An Extract from a Session

Patient M was on time and pressed the buzzer very lightly.

She was silent for about five minutes. Then she said it was only when she was leaving at the end of the last session that she was able to start crying – when she got to the lift. In the session itself she had felt that nothing had happened. She said she did not want to be here today. What she wanted to say before she came here she did not want to say now. She said there was nothing happening.

She then told me about watching a programme about men and women who are frightened of putting on weight on television the night before. Most of them were anorexics, but there was one bulimic. She said that when she binged she imagined that she would put on stones and stones of weight overnight. She added that she was beginning to feel that way again, that she was becoming obsessed about food and that she worried about putting on weight and that she wanted to start making herself sick again. She said she didn't know how she ever lived with herself when she was making herself sick all the time, every day and taking laxatives. She had stopped vomiting when she went to India but she had eaten all the time there, whenever she could, anyway. She did not know whether she would have stopped being sick if she had not gone to India. She said it was just the same as when she started coming here – thinking about food all the time, feeling this way, she does not know what else is wrong with her. A short pause then followed. She said, 'When I think of my mother and sister, they don't worry any more, because I'm not being sick and vomiting. I'm thinking about going home at Christmas.'

She said that because she was eating like this she thought there was something that she really did not want to face up to, rather than worrying about changing jobs and going to interviews, that there must be more. She said,

> You're making me feel like this. I'm wondering why whenever I see an upset child in the cinema I feel like crying, I feel so bad about myself. I saw this article about a guy who was an alcoholic. I was admiring his ability to change himself so much. I can't even make a small change. I'm dreading Christmas. I'm just going to eat, feel so alone.

I said, 'I think you feel alone when you're here at the moment and even more alone when you leave here. The Christmas break is coming up: I think you feel I've abandoned you already.'

She started to sob quite hard and then said that she had been thinking about whether she had changed or not, that all the changes are negative ones, that she is more outspoken at work, that she nags them, gives out to them all of the time, that she involves herself with bitchiness, that she is more social with people at work – but that it is in a bad way.

I said, 'You're disappointed and want "to give out" to me for not having helped you more.'

She said she thought that I knew what it was, that I knew what the problem was, and that she wanted to know why nothing changes. It is just the same month after month and that I wanted her to figure it out and she never will.

I said, 'You feel I'm keeping secrets from you, that I have the answers and that I'm not letting you in on them.'

She said that I was some kind of a trained counsellor and that I was meant to know the stages of getting better. She wants to move house. She does not really get on that well with her flatmate, R, that they were never really that close. It was just like it had been in the last place, when she stayed with people in Boston, that she never kept in touch with anyone from then.

She then gave a big sigh.

She was thinking about going to the second interview and how she had to change the time of her session and leave early. This was followed quickly by her saying that she did not understand why she thinks about so many things when she is here. She said she thought she was just thinking about all of these things to avoid what is really upsetting her. She cannot think of anything, that she is numbed from eating, that all she thinks about is stupid things, that she does not even know what it is that is upsetting her so much.

I said, 'Are you going to give it a guess?'

She went straight off at a trot, eagerly:

I must have been really unhappy when I was younger. I don't understand how come my sisters aren't like me. I don't know what I picked up to make me feel like this. I suppose when I think about something being wrong with me, I think of something that must have happened a long time ago – that it's very deep. I want desperately to remember more, but I feel like I'm choosing to forget more. I never seem to think about my father. I forget about being bulimic, what it was really like, forget what it was like when I came back from Boston and spent five weeks in Maidenhead – that it was a job I hated. I lived with an elderly couple. I can't even remember their names or the names of the people who shared the house with them. I'll never be able to figure it out, because I remember nothing.

She continued by saying she supposed it was that she was thinking about how unsociable she feels, that she does not want to go out with her flatmate R. R had gone out the night before and M had decided not to go out with her. She had gone out the previous week with T, but had not really wanted to. It is not okay when she's binge eating. She does not want to ask anyone to supper; she is 'too depressed, wrapped up in myself to bother about other people'. She then said she wanted to be left alone but that she also did not want to be, and that she felt her life would never improve 'if I keep shutting myself off from people'. She spoke about a woman at the agency, who was confident and enthusiastic – that she must think that M was a pathetic person, that she was so childish. The same kind of thing happens in her French class, where she also feels childish and useless.

I said, 'So you're managing not to shut yourself off from people, although it's hard. You're going to your French class, going to the agency, beginning to wonder about the past: your father, your bulimia, your childhood – and you're feeling very aware of how you feel.'

She asked me repeat what I had said and I did.

She then said that a friend at work had asked her what colour hair her parents had and she didn't know what colour hair her father had. She just remembered that it was grey, that she hadn't any idea what colour it was before that. It was the anniversary of his death on 10 November.

M was in the middle of a binge when she came to her session and the words flowed towards me in a violent and attacking stream. If my first interpretation had addressed her way of relating, or the rage she was feeling, she would have denied it and would probably have withdrawn. It would have been experienced as a reprojection of her own feelings, regardless of how it was said. Underneath her rage with me was an awareness of a holiday break coming up and the hopeless feelings she had inside. By addressing her feelings of being alone in the session, when she was with me, feelings which became even worse when she was away from me, and linking this to her feeling that I had already left her for the break, I was able to make a connection with her. She started to sob and a point of contact was made. This was immediately followed by a more concentrated attack on the work we did together and how I had just made her into a 'nasty' person.

The initial tirade had been intense and provoked a conscious wish in me to retaliate. I did not do so, but by the tone and language of my next interpretation I very much played on her wish that I should attack her. Her own ferocity was reduced, and although her words may appear somewhat attacking in the transcript of the session itself, I was aware of feeling increasingly angry as she became less so. The pitfalls of remaining silent in this instance are that with this particular patient withdrawal is taken to be an aggressive act, and it would have simply confirmed her feeling of being abandoned. I struggled internally with how to transform my wish to get inside her, to affect her, to stop her being angry, to stop my anger by hurting her. Thinking about space and where and how to place an interpretation, I decided I needed to create a space between us so that we did not get into a downward spiral of attack and withdrawal (see Wilson and Sohn above, pp. 69–70). I said, 'Are you going to give it a guess?' in a light and non-persecutory or sharp tone of voice, which meant that she could find her own voice. The session shifted from that point on. It shifted into rich, but confusing material, mixes of old and new, coming out in a higgledy-piggledy way. It felt like friendly and bewildering vomit which I had to hold and not interpret. I understood some of it, the familiar strands, but my role was not to ask questions about it. It had to be accepted and contained, not interpreted or reprojected. I think her wish for me to repeat what I said near the end of the session was because my words were so at variance with the expected internal attack, which seemed clearly represented in the story of the woman at the agency who was confident and able and who therefore would believe M to be stupid, useless and childish. The not-hearing could be seen as both a defence against an expected attack and also a defence against helpful or understanding words which might need to be attacked to prevent her then feeling diminished. I think her asking for them a second time suggested a wish to hear, to not be knocked out by them, or to knock me out by not hearing them, for them to be allowed to exist as something good.

It was a major shift that she was beginning to bring her rage and distress to the session, after some years of severe depression and suicidal feelings. She was a very powerful woman who often made thought impossible during sessions. She would often, as Marie Maguire's patient did, project so powerfully that I experienced an inability to think and make sense during sessions, so that sometimes a large portion of a session would disappear into a vague dreamscape. The concrete nature and strength of her projective identifications becomes easier to think about and understand using ideas of intermediate and transitional objects.

M, like so many bulimics, does not have an in-between: she takes over, or she is taken over. There is in many senses only one area of experiencing, that of her own internal world. There seem to be only two choices in her world, either being engulfed or engulfing, or abandoned and abandoning. I have to exist in the sessions in a transitional space to help my patients find it within themselves and to avoid the enticements of narcissistic collusion.

By this I mean that many bulimics and anorexics can talk away happily and give the appearance of making progress, whereas they are often unconsciously being the intermediate object for the therapist, who feels very good about the work, and perhaps the closeness of the fit between herself and the patient. By this I mean they are unconsciously picking up the imagined signals of the therapist and giving her or him just what they want. This is how the patient behaved with her mother and continues to behave with her internal mother. This is repeated in the transference where she perceives herself as being purely an extension of the therapist. Anorexics and bulimics protect themselves from the perceived horrors of being known, and it is essential to be aware of this if they are going to be helped and to recognise and address their terror of experiencing a repetition of being uncontained and their material being indigestible.

Final Thoughts

Hilde Bruch was very aware of the tremendous fragility of her anorexic patients, and her active approach was designed to contain and to help them. I think it can be replaced by a less directive, but equally active approach. That is, by actively using the dynamic of the transference and countertransference to make interpretations, which do 'contain' annihilatory and separation anxieties. What I have not spoken of directly is the technical difference between working with anorexics, anorexic bulimics and normal weight bulimics. This involves an inappropriate amount of generalisation – but moves along a familiar trajectory. One of the main differences is the unconscious death wishes of the anorexic versus the more conscious ones of the bulimic. In practice, this makes the anorexic harder to reach with interpretations, as they have invested so much in their wish *not* to exist. Bulimics are more likely to throw interpretations up, unless presented in a non-threatening and digestible way, their ambivalence and wish for relationships parallels their relationship to food.

This leads to the next distinction, between those who binge and those who do not. The dynamic is similar but with the anorexic bulimics the presence of much stronger self-destructive tendencies and the wish to use food to abuse, not to nourish, makes them the hardest group to work with. Normal weight bulimics are the group most able to use the therapist and the therapeutic space as a play room, a place where intermediate and eventually transitional objects, in the form of interpretations, may be found and put to good use. They are found in the interaction between therapist and patient. For all eating disordered patients interpretations will often feel invasive or penetrative. When this is the case, an anorexic often responds with an enraged 'no' and a bulimic with a greedy 'yes' with the subsequent wish to get rid of the interpretation. This is the norm and needs to be appreciated, so that the lack of movement can be tolerated and interpretations can then, for many become 'edible'.

CHAPTER 5

Conclusion

I have tried to elucidate the emergence of eating disorders, since the eleventh century, paying particular attention to the psychoanalytic meaning of the symptom, whether it be anorexic or bulimic. I have attempted to differentiate anorexics from anorexic bulimics and normal weight bulimics, and have done so mainly on the premise of weight, but also on the presence or absence of the bulimic symptom. The symptoms were originally understood as a complex defence against positive and then negative Oedipal wishes. The ego psychologists in the United States became more interested in the early separation–individuation struggles of these patients, and the Kleinians, entering the same developmental period from their particular perspective, saw the problems as being narcissistic, and focused particularly on the role of envy in these patients.

In the chapter on transitional objects I raised the issue of the mother's own pathology and her desire not to know her child, as well as her wish to use her for her own purposes and to the child's detriment. This can be seen with anorexics whose way of life is designed to preserve the idea that their own life, their very existence, should not be a matter for concern. It is also paralleled in the bulimic ritual itself by taking in too much food which cannot be nourishing and has to be expelled. It may also be a child's only experience of connecting with mother, however briefly, and I have argued that it is this moment of re-enacted connection which enables bulimic individuals to use the post-binge period as a transitional time, when vomit or the rituals around clearing up are used as transitional phenomena. Bulimics attempt to use the vomit as a transitional, rather than intermediate object, and this is possible after a binge, when the echo of a good experience of mother is still internally available.

In Chapter 4 I wanted to use these ideas to try to understand the extreme difficulties of working with this group of patients – difficulties that mean that many psychotherapists were opposed to psychoanalytic work with these patients altogether, or at least not until they had put on weight. Bruch (1978), Palazzoli (1978) and the self psychologists put forward a variety of more active styles. The neutrality and abstinence of the therapeutic space was felt to be intolerable by these patients and – I would also like to add – by their therapists. By looking at the unconscious power of mother's impact on the child I hope to move the focus from patient to therapist so that working in the countertransference becomes *the* way to work with these patients. A way to understand the power of the feelings evoked in the countertransference is to think about the very early separation difficulties and particularly about the possibility of mother having attempted to use her child as an intermediate object.

What is then necessary in the therapeutic relationship is to allow the patient to use the therapist as an intermediate object and for the therapist to provide an effective experience of a transitional space in which patient and therapist can work together. Perhaps the storms in the therapy, the attacks made by bulimics on the therapist, can be understood as an attempt to revive a link and, once this has been survived, work can take place in the transitional space; in the aftermath of the bingeing, in the acceptance of the vomit, sometimes projectile, that occurs within the therapeutic relationship. The vomit has to be accepted as a gift and like a transitional object must be not questioned, or taken away, until its use has faded into insignificance. Metaphorical vomiting is being used in the therapeutic relationship as a way of creating a space in which to work, which has to be understood and protected if these patients are to move towards whole object relationships. This move in turn facilitates the existence of an effective digestive tract in their internal world and internal objects which at last can tolerate the digestive process.

References

Abraham, K. (1916) 'The First Pregenital Stage of the Libido', in *Selected Papers of Karl Abraham*. London: Karnac, 1979, reprinted 1988, pp. 248–79.

—— (1924) 'Development of the Libido', in *Selected Papers of Karl Abraham*. London: Karnac, 1979, reprinted 1988, pp. 418–501.

Balint, E. (1993) *Before I Was I: Psychoanalysis and the Imagination*. London: Free Association Books.

Barret, D. and Fine, H. J. (1990) 'The Gnostic Syndrome: Anorexia Nervosa', *Psychoanalytic Psychotherapy* 4: 263–70.

Bell, R. M. (1985) *Holy Anorexia*. Chicago: University of Chicago Press.

Bion, W. (1962) *Learning from Experience*. London: Heinemann.

Binswanger, L. (1944) 'The Case of Ellen West', in Rollo May, ed., *Existence: A New Dimension in Psychiatry and Psychology*. New York: Basic Books, 1958.

Bird, B. (1957) 'A specific Peculiarity of Acting Out', *Journal of the American Psychoanalytic Association* 1: 630–47.

Birksted-Breen, D. (1989) 'Working with an Anorexic Patient', *International Journal of Psycho-Analysis* 70: 29–40.

Blos, P. (1974) 'The Geneology of the Ego Ideal', *The Psychoanalytic Study of the Child* 29: 43–88.

Boris, H. N. (1984a) 'The Problem of Anorexia Nervosa', *International Journal of Psycho-Analysis* 65: 315–22.

—— (1984b) 'On the Treatment of Anorexia Nervosa', *International Journal of Psycho-Analysis* 65: 435–42.

—— (1988) 'Torment of the Object: A Contribution to the Study of Bulimia', in H. J. Schwartz, ed. (1988b), pp. 89–111.

Boskind-White, M. and White, W. C. (1987) *Bulimarexia: The Binge/Purge Cycle.* New York: Norton, reprinted 1991.

Bovey, S. (1989) *Being Fat Is Not a Sin.* London: Pandora.

Brenman Pick, I. (1985) 'Working Through in the Countertransference', *International Journal of Psycho-Analysis* 66: 157–66.

Brenner, C. (1974) 'The Concept of Phenomenology of Depression With Special Reference to the Aged', *Journal of Geriatric Psychiatry* 7: 6–20.

Brenner, D. (1983) 'Self-Regulatory Functions in Bulimia', *Contempory Psychotherapy Review* 1: 79–96.

Bruch, H. (1962) 'Perceptual and Conceptual Disturbances in Anorexia Nervosa', *Psychosomatic Medicine* 24: 187–94.

—— (1965) 'Anorexia Nervosa and Its Differential Diagnosis', *Journal of Nervous and Mental Diseases* 141: 555–6.

—— (1970) 'Psychotherapy in Primary Anorexia Nervosa', *Journal of Nervous and Mental Diseases* 105: 51–67.

—— (1973) *Eating Disorders: Obesity, Anorexia and the Person Within.* New York: Basic Books.

—— (1974) 'Perils of Behaviour Modification in the Treatment of Anorexia Nervosa', *Journal of the American Medical Association* 230: 1409–22.

—— (1978) *The Golden Cage: The Enigma of Anorexia Nervosa.* Cambridge, Massachusetts: Harvard University Press.

—— (1985) 'Four Decades of Eating Disorders', in D. M. Garner and P. E. Garfinkel, eds (1985), pp. 7–19.

Brumberg, J. J. (1988) *Fasting Girls: The Emergence of Anorexia Nervosa as a Modern Disease.* Cambridge, Massachusetts: Harvard University Press.

Brunswick, R. M. (1940) 'The Preoedipal Phase of Libido Development', in R. Fliess, ed. *The Psychoanalytic Reader.* New York: International Universities Press, pp. 261–83.

Bynum, C. W. (1987) *Holy Feast and Holy Fast: The Religious Significance of Food to Medieval Women.* Berkeley: University of California Press.

Cannon, G. and Einseg, H. (1983) *Stop Dieting Because Dieting Makes You Fat.* New York: Simon and Schuster.

Casper, R. C., Eckert, E. D., Halmi, K. A., Goldberg, S. and Davis, J. M. (1980) 'Bulimia: Its Incidence and

Clinical Importance in Patients with Anorexia Nervosa', *Archives of General Psychiatry* 37: 1030–5.

Charcot, J.-M. (1889) *Diseases of the Nervous System*, III. London: The New Sydenham Society.

Chernin, K. (1983) *Womansize: The Tyranny of Slenderness*. London: The Women's Press.

Coles, P. (1988) 'Aspects of Perversion in Anorexic Bulimic Disorders', *Psychoanalytic Psychotherapy* 3: 137–49.

Coward, R. (1993) *Our Treacherous Hearts*. London: Faber and Faber.

Crisp, A. H. (1965) 'Clinical and Therapeutic Aspects of Anorexia Nervosa: A Study of 30 Cases', *Journal of Psychosomatic Research* 9: 67.

—— (1967) 'Anorexia Nervosa', *Hospital Medicine* 1: 713–18.

—— (1968) 'Primary Anorexia Nervosa', *Gut* 9: 370–2.

—— (1980) *Anorexia Nervosa: Let Me Be*. New York: Academic Press.

—— and Toms, D. A. (1972) 'Primary Anorexia Nervosa or Weight Phobia in the Male', *British Medical Journal* 1: 334–8.

Cross, L. W. (1993) 'Body and Self in Feminine Development: Implications for Eating Disorders and Delicate Self-Mutilation', *Bulletin of the Menninger Clinic* 57: 41–63.

Dally, P. J. (1969) *Anorexia Nervosa*. New York: Grune and Stratton.

—— (1989) Personal communication.

Dare, C. (1993) 'Aetiological Models and the Psychotherapy of Psychosomatic Disorders', in M. Hodes and S. Moorey, eds, *Psychological Treatment in Disease and Illness*. London: The Society for Psychosomatic Research, pp. 9–30.

Deutsch, H (1930) 'The Significance of Masochism in the Mental Life of Women', in R. Fliess, ed. (1948) pp. 223–36.

—— (1932) 'On Female Homosexuality', in R. Fliess, ed. (1948) pp. 237–60.

—— (1944) *The Psychology of Women: A Psychoanalytic Interpretation*. Volume 1, New York: Grune and Stratton.

—— (1945) *The Psychology of Women: A Psychoanalytic Interpretation*. Volume 2, New York: Grune and Stratton.

Doctors, S. (1979) *The Symptom of Delicate Self-Cutting in Adolescent Females: A Developmental View*. Unpublished doctoral dissertation, Yeshiva University, New York City.

DSM-I: (1952), *Diagnostic and Statistical Manual of Mental Disorder*. Washington, D.C.: American Psychiatric Association.

DSM-II: (1968), *Diagnostic and Statistical Manual of Mental Disorder*, 2nd ed. Washington, D.C.: American Psychiatric Association.

DSM-III-R: (1988), *Diagnostic and Statistical Manual of Mental Disorder*, 3rd ed., revised. Washington, D.C.: American Psychiatric Association.

Duker, M. and Slade, R. (1988) *Anorexia Nervosa and Bulimia: How To Help*. Philadelphia: Open University Press.

Dunbar, M. (1987) *Catherine: The Story of a Young Girl Who Died of Anorexia*. Harmondsworth: Penguin.

Eliot, T. S. (1917) 'The Love Song of J. Alfred Prufrock', in *The Complete Poems and Plays of T. S. Eliot*. London: Faber and Faber, 1969.

Fairburn, C. G. (1981) 'A Cognitive-Behavioural Approach to the Management of Bulimia', *Psychological Medicine* 141: 631–3.

—— (1982) *Binge-eating and Bulimia Nervosa*. London: Smith, Kline and French.

Felton, O. (1994) Private communication.

Fenichel, O. (1945) 'Anorexia', in H. Fenichel, ed. *The Collected Papers of Otto Fenichel*. New York: Norton, 1954, pp. 296–304.

Fliess, R., ed. (1948) *The Psychoanalytic Reader*. New York: International Universities Press.

Fraiberg, S. (1972) 'Some Characteristics of Genital Arousal and Discharge in Latency Girls', *The Psychoanalytic Study of the Child* 27: 439–75.

Freud A. (1937) *The Ego and the Mechanisms of Defence*, trans. C. Baines. London: Hogarth Press, 1936.

Freud, S. (1899) 'Extracts from the Fliess Papers', in James Strachey, ed. *The Standard Edition of the Complete Psychological Works of Sigmund Freud*, 24 vols, Hogarth, 1953–73. Vol. 1, pp. 175–280.

—— (1931) 'Female Sexuality', *S. E.* 21, pp. 225–43.

—— (1905) *Three Essays on the Theory of Sexuality. S. E.* 7, pp. 125–249.

Gabbard, G. O. (1989) 'On "Doing Nothing" in the Psychoanalytic Treatment of the Refractory Borderline Patient', *International Journal of Psycho-Analysis* 70: 527–34.

—— (1990) *Psychodynamic Psychiatry in Clinical Practice.* Washington, D.C.: American Psychiatric Association Press.

Ganzarain, R. C. and Buchele, B. J. (1988) *Fugitives of Incest: A Perspective from Psychoanalysis and Groups.* Madison, Connecticut: International Universities Press.

Garner, D. and Garfinkel, P., eds (1982) 'Hospital Management', in *Anorexia Nervosa, A Multidimensional Perspective.* New York: Brunner/Mazel, pp. 216–57.

—— eds (1985) *Handbook of Psychotherapy for Anorexia Nervosa and Bulimia.* London: Guilford Press.

Gehrie, M. (1990) 'Eating Disorders and Adaptation in Crisis: An Hypothesis', *American Psychiatric Press Annual Review of Psychiatry* 9: 369–83.

Geist, R. A. (1985) 'Therapeutic Dilemmas in the Treatment of Anorexia Nervosa: A Self-Psychological Perspective', in S. W. Emmet, ed., *Theory and Treatment of Anorexia Nervosa and Bulimia: Biomedical, Sociocultural, and Psychological Perspectives.* New York: Brunner/Mazel, pp. 268–88.

Goodsitt, A. (1983) 'Self-Regulatory Disturbances in Eating Disorders', *International Journal of Eating Disorders* 2: 51–60.

—— (1985) 'Self Psychology and the Treatment of Anorexia Nervosa', in D. M. Garner and P. E. Garfinkel, eds (1985), pp. 55–83.

Green, A. (1977) 'Conceptions of Affect', *International Journal of Psycho-Analysis* 58: 129–56.

Greenacre, P. (1950) 'Special Problems of Early Female Sexual Development', *The Psychoanalytic Study of the Child* 5: 122–38.

—— (1952) 'Anatomical Structure and Superego Development', in *Trauma, Growth and Personality.* New York: International Universities Press, 1971, pp. 149–64.

Gull W. W. (1873) 'Apepsia Hysterica: Anorexia Hysterica', *Transcripts of the Clinical Society of London* 7: 22–8.

Hartman, H. (1958) *Ego Psychology and the Problem of Adaptation*, trans. by D. Rappaport. New York: International Universities Press.

Hogan, C. C. (1983) 'Object Relations', in Wilson *et al.* (1985), pp.129–52.

—— (1985) 'Technical Problems in Psychoanalytic Treatment', in Wilson *et al.* (1985), pp. 197–215.

—— (1992) 'The Adolescent Crisis in Anorexia Nervosa', in Wilson *et al.* (1992), pp. 111–29.

Hsu, G. L .K. (1986) 'The Treatment of Anorexia Nervosa', *American Journal of Psychiatry* 143: 573–81.

Hsu, G. L. K. (1990) *Eating Disorders.* New York: Guilford.

Isaacs, S. (1948) 'The Nature and Function of Phantasy', *International Journal of Psycho-Analysis* 29: 73–97.

Janet, P. (1929) *The Major Symptoms of Hysteria.* New York: Macmillan, quoted in R. M. Kaufman and M. Heiman, eds (1964), pp. 156–60.

Jessner, L. and Abse, D. (1960) 'Regressive Forces in Anorexia Nervosa', *British Journal of Medical Psychology* 33: 301–12.

Johnson, C. L. (1991a) 'Treatment of Eating-Disordered Patients with Borderline and False-Self/Narcissistic Disorders', in C. L. Johnson, ed. (1991b), pp. 165–93.

—— ed. (1991b) *Psychodynamic Treatment of Anorexia Nervosa and Bulimia.* New York: Guilford.

Johnson, C. and Conners, M. E. (1987) *The Etiology and Treatment of Bulimia Nervosa.* New York: Basic Books.

Jones, E. (1927) 'The Early Development of Female Sexuality', *International Journal of Psycho-Analysis* 8: 459–72.

Karol, C. (1980) 'The Role of Primal Scene and Masochism in Asthma', *International Journal of Psychoanalytic Psychotherapy* 8: 577–92.

Kaufman, R. M. and Heiman, M., eds (1964) *Evolution of Psychosomatic Concepts. Anorexia Nervosa: A Paradigm.* New York: International Universities Press.

Kestenberg, J. (1968) 'Outside and Inside, Male and Female', *Journal of American Psychoanalytic Association* 16: 457–520.

—— (1970) 'Discussion of Greenacre's paper "The Transitional Object and the Fetish: Special Reference to the Role of Illusion"', meeting of the New York Psychoanalytic Society, 17 March.

—— and Weinstein, J. (1988) 'Transitional Objects and Body-Image Formation', in Grolnick *et al.*, eds (1988) *Between Reality and Phantasy: Winnicott's Concepts of Transitional Objects and Phenomena*. New York: Jason Aronson, pp. 75–97.

Klein, M. (1920) 'The Development of a Child', *International Journal of Psycho-Analysis* 4: 419–74.

—— (1923) 'The Role of the School in the Libidinal Development of the Child', *International Journal of Psycho-Analysis* 5: 312–31.

—— (1925) 'A Contribution to the Psychogenesis of Tics', in *Contributions to Psycho-Analysis*. London: Hogarth, pp.117–39.

—— (1946) 'Notes on Some Schizoid Mechanisms', *International Journal of Psychoanalysis*, 27: 99–100.

Klein, S. (1980) 'Autistic Phenomena in Neurotic Patients', *International Journal of Psycho-Analysis* 61: 395–401.

Kohut, H. (1971) *The Analysis of the Self*. New York: Basic Books.

Kris, E. (1950) 'The Significance of Freud's Earliest Discoveries', *International Journal of Psycho-Analysis* 31: 108–16.

Krueger, D. and Schofield, E. (1987) 'An Integration of Verbal and Nonverbal Therapies is Disorders of the Self', *Journal of Arts in Psychotherapy* 13: 323–31.

Krueger, D. W. (1988) 'Body Self, Psychological Self, and Bulimia: Developmental and Clinical Considerations', in Schwartz, ed. (1988b), pp. 55–73.

—— (1990) 'Developmental and Psychodynamic Perspectives of Body-Image Change', in T. F. Cash and T. Pruzinsky, eds, *Body Images: Development, Deviance, and Change*. New York: Guilford, pp. 255–71.

Lampl-de Groot, J. (1927) 'The Evolution of the Oedipus Complex in Women', *International Journal of Psycho-Analysis* 9: 332–45.

Lasègue, C. (1873) 'De l'anorexie hysterique', *Archives Generales de Medicine*. Reprinted in R. M. Kaufman and M. Heiman, eds (1964), pp. 141–55.

Laufer, E. (1991) 'Body Image, Sexuality and the Psychotic Core', *International Journal of Psycho-Analysis* 72: 63–73.

Lautenbacher, S., Galfe, G., Hoelzl, R. and Prike, K. M. (1989) 'Gastrointestinal Transit Is Delayed in Patients with Bulimia', *International Journal of Eating Disorders* 8: 203–8.

Lawrence, M., ed. (1987) *Fed Up and Hungry: Women, Oppression and Food*. London: The Women's Press, reprinted 1989, 1992, 1994.

Leonard, C. E. (1944) 'An Analysis of a Case of Functional Vomiting and Bulimia', *Psychoanalytic Review* 31: 1–18.

Lerner, H. D. (1983) 'Contempory Psychoanalytic Perspectives on Gorge Vomiting: A Case Illustration', *International Journal of Eating Disorders* 3: 47–63.

—— (1993) 'Masochism in Subclinical Eating Disorders', in C. L. Johnson, ed. (1991), pp. 110–27.

Lewin, B. D. (1933) 'The Body as Phallus', *Psychoanalytic Quarterly* 2: 24–47.

Lorand, S. (1943) 'Anorexia Nervosa', *Psychosomatic Medicine* 5: 282–92.

Lowenstein, R. M. (1951) 'Freud: Man and Scientist', *Bulletin of the New York Academy of Medicine* 27: 623–37.

McDougall, J. (1989) *Theatres of the Body: A Psychoanalytic Approach to Psychosomatic Illness*. London: Free Association Books.

MacKensie, S. (1888) 'On a Case of Anorexia Vel Hysterica', *Lancet* 1: 613–14.

Maguire, M. (1989) 'Pornography and Bulimia: Gender and the Denial of Psychic Reality', in B. Richards, ed. (1989) *Crises of the Self: Further Essays on Psychoanalysis and Politics*. London: Free Association Books, pp. 113–27.

Mahler, M., Pine, F. and Bergman, A. (1975) *The Psychological Birth of the Human Infant*. London: Hutchinson.

Masserman, J. H. (1941) 'Psychodynamics in Anorexia Nervosa and Neurotic Vomiting', *Psychoanalytic Quarterly* 10: 211–42.

Minuchin, S. (1974) *Families and Family Therapy.* Cambridge, Massachusetts: Harvard University Press.

Morton, R. (1689) *Pathisologica or a Treatise on Consumption.* London: Smith and Walford.

Moulton, R. (1942) 'A Psychosomatic Study of Anorexia Nervosa Including the Use of Vaginal Smears', *Psychosomatic Medicine* 4: 62–74.

Mushatt, C. (1992) 'Anorexia Nervosa as an Expression of Ego-Defective Development', in Wilson *et al.*, eds. (1992), pp. 301–11.

Nagera, H. (1975) *Female Sexuality and the Oedipus Complex.* New York: Jason Aronson.

Nandeau (1789) 'Observation sur une Maladie Nerveuse Accompagnée d'un Dégout Extraordinaire pour les Ailments', *Journal de Médicine Chirurgie et Pharmacologie* 8: 197–201.

Neubauer, P. B. (1960) 'The One Parent Child and His Oedipal Development', *Psychoanalytic Study of the Child* 15, 286–309.

Novick, J. and Novick, K. K. (1991) 'Some Comments on Masochism and the Delusion of Omnipotence from a Developmental Perspective', *Journal of the American Psychoanalytic Association* 39: 307–31.

Orbach, S. (1979) *Fat Is a Feminist Issue: The Anti-Diet Guide to Permanent Weight Loss.* London: Hamlyn.

Osler, W. (1892) *Principles of Practice of Medicine.* New York: Appleton.

—— (1912) *The Principles and Practice of Medicine.* New York and London: D. Appleton and Co.

Oxford English Dictionary (1961) Oxford: Clarendon Press.

Palazzoli, M. S. (1978) *Self-Starvation: From Individual to Family Therapy in the Treatment of Anorexia Nervosa.* New York: Jason Aronson.

Parry Jones, B. and Parry Jones, W. L. (1991) 'Bulimia: An Archival Review of Its History in Psychosomatic Medicine', *International Journal of Eating Disorders* 10: 129–43.

Pines, D. (1993) *A Woman's Unconscious Use of Her Body: A Psychoanalytical Understanding.* London: Virago.

Rappaport, D. (1960) 'The Structure of Psychoanalytic Theory: A Systematizing Attempt', *Psychological Issues* 2, Monograph 6.

Reifenstien, E. C. (1946). 'Psychogenic or "Hypothalmic Amenorrhea"', *Medical Clinics of North America* 30: 1103–21.

Reiser, L. W. (1990) 'The Oral Triad and the Bulimic Quintet: Understanding the Bulimic Episode', *International Review of Psycho-Analysis* 17: 238–48.

Riddle, H. H., ed. (1914) *The Family Encyclopaedia of Medicine.* London: Amalgamated Press.

Ritvo, S. (1984) 'The Image and Uses of the Body in Psychic Conflict: With Special Reference to Eating Disorders in Adolescence', *Psychoanalytic Study of the Child* 39: 449–70.

Rizzuto, A.-M. (1988) 'Transference, Language and Affect in the Treatment of Bulimarexia', *International Journal of Psycho-Analysis* 69: 369–87.

Rosenfeld, H. (1971) 'A Clinical Approach to the Psychoanalytic Theory of the Life and Death Instincts: An Investigation into the Aggressive Aspects of Narcissism', *International Journal of Psycho-Analysis* 52: 169–78.

Russell, G. (1979) 'Bulimia Nervosa: An Ominous Variant of Anorexia Nervosa', *Psychological Medicine* 9: 429–48.

Ryle, A. (1936) 'Anorexia Nervosa', *Lancet* 2: 892–4.

Sands, S. (1991) 'Bulimia, Dissociation and Empathy: A Self-Psychological View', in C. L. Johnson, ed. (1991), pp. 34–51.

Sarnoff, C. (1983) 'Derivatives of Latency', in Wilson *et al.*, eds. (1985), pp. 327–34.

Schwartz, H. (1986) 'Bulimia: Psychoanalytic Perspectives', *Journal of the American Psychoanalytic Association* 34: 439–67.

—— (1988a) 'Bulimia: Psychoanalytic Perspectives', in H. J. Schwartz, ed. (1988b), pp. 31–55.

—— ed. (1988b) *Bulimia: Psychoanalytic Treatment and Theory.* Connecticut: International Universities Press.

Shulman, D. (1991) 'A Multitiered View of Bulimia', *International Journal of Eating Disorders* 10: 333–43.

Simmonds, M. (1914) 'Ueber Hypophysisschwund mit todlichem Ausgang', *Deutsche Medizinische Wochenschrift* 1: 322–3.

—— (1916) 'Ueber Kachexie hypophysaren Ursprungs', *Deutsche Medizinische Wochenschrift* 1: 190–1.

Sohn, L. (1985) 'Anorexic and Bulimic States of Mind in the Psycho-Analytic Treatment of Anorexic/Bulimic Patients and Psychotic Patients', *Psychoanalytic Psychotherapy* 1: 49–56.

Sollier, P. (1891) 'Anorexie Hystérique (Sitiergie Hystérique)', *Revue Medicale* 2: 625–50.

Soltman, O. (1894) 'Anorexia cerebralis und centrale nutritionsneurose', *Jahbuch der Kinderheilklinik* 38: 1–13.

Sours, J. (1974) 'The Anorexia Nervosa Syndrome', *International Journal of Psycho-Analysis*, 55: 567–76.

—— (1980) *Starving To Death in a Sea of Objects.* New York: Jason Aronson.

Sperling. M. (1949) 'The Role of the Mother in Psychosomatic Disorders in Children', *Psychosomatic Medicine* 11: 377–85.

—— (1968) 'Trichotillomania, Trichophagy and Cyclic Vomiting', *International Journal of Psycho-Analysis* 49: 682–90.

—— (1973) 'Conversion Hysteria and Conversion Symptoms: A Revision of Classification and Concepts', *Journal of American Psychoanalytic Association* 21: 745–71.

—— (1978) 'Case Histories of Anorexia Nervosa', in *Psychosomatic Disorders in Childhood.* New York: Jason Aronson, pp. 139–73.

—— (1983) 'A Reevaluation of Classification, Concepts and Treatment', in Wilson *et al.*, eds (1985), pp. 51–82.

Sperling, O. (1943–45) 'On Appersonation', *International Journal of Psycho-Analysis* 24–26: 128–32.

Sprince, M. (1984) 'Early Psychic Disturbances in Anorexic and Bulimic Patients as Reflected in the Analytic Process', *Journal of Child Psychotherapy* 10: 199–216.

Sprince, M. P. (1988) 'Experiencing and Recovering Transitional Space in the Analytic Treatment of Anorexia Nervosa and Bulimia', in H. J. Schwartz, ed. (1988b), pp. 73–89.

Stangler, R. S. and Prinz, A. M. (1980) 'DSM-III: Psychiatric Diagnosis in a University Population', *American Journal of Psychiatry* 137: 937–40.

Steiner, J. (1993) *Psychic Retreats: Pathological Organisations in Psychotic, Neurotic and Borderline Patients.* London: Routledge.

Stunkard, A. J., Grace, W. J. and Woff, H. G. (1955) 'The Night Eating Syndrome: A Pattern of Food Intake Among Certain Obese Patients', *American Journal of Medicine* 19: 78–86.

Sugarman, A. (1991) 'Bulimia: A Displacement from Psychological Self to Body Self', in C. L. Johnson, ed. (1991), pp. 3–34.

—— and Kurash, C. (1982) 'The Body as a Transitional Object in Bulimia', *International Journal of Eating Disorders* 1 : 57–67.

Swift, W. J. and Letven, R. (1984) 'Bulimia and the Basic Fault: A Psychoanalytic Interpretation of the Binging-Vomiting Syndrome', *Journal of the American Academy of Child Psychiatry* 23: 489–97.

Sylvester, E. (1945) 'Analysis of Psychogenic Anorexia and Vomiting in a Four-Year-Old Child', *The Psychoanalytic Study of the Child* 2: 3–16.

Tedesco, P. C. and Reisen, S. E. (1985) 'Anorexia Nervosa: Theory and Therapy – A New Look at an Old Problem', *Journal of the American Psychoanalytic Association* 36: 153–161.

Thöma, H. (1967) *Anorexia Nervosa.* New York: International Universities Press.

Tourette, G. Gilles de la (1895) *Traité Clinique et Thérapeutique de l'Hystérie*, 3rd ed. Paris: Plor Nourit.

Tyson, P. and Tyson, R. (1990) *Psychoanalytic Theories of Development: An Integration.* New Haven, Connecticut: Yale University Press.

Waller, J. V., Kaufman, M. R. and Deutsch, F. (1940) 'Anorexia Nervosa: A Psychosomatic Entity', in M. R. Kaufman and M. Heiman, eds (1964), pp. 145–276.

Whytt, R. (1767) *Observations on the Nature, Causes and Cures of Those Disorders Which Have Been Commonly Called Nervous, Hypochondriac or Hysteric: To Which Are Prefixed*

Some Remarks on the Sympathy of the Nerves. London: Becket and de Hondt.

Williams, G. (1994) Communication in the Eating Disorders Workshop at the Tavistock Clinic, London.

Wilson, C. P. (1982) 'Fifteen-Year Follow Up on a Case of Ulcerative Colitis', case presentation to the Psychoanalytic Discussion Group of the Psychoanalytic Association of New York, 14 February.

—— (1983) 'Fat Phobia as a Diagnostic Term To Replace a Medical Misnomer: Anorexia Nervosa', paper presented to a meeting of the American Academy of Child Psychiatry, October, San Francisco.

—— (1985) 'Contrast in the Analysis of Bulimic and Abstaining Anorexics' in Wilson *et al.*, eds (1985), pp. 169–93.

—— (1986) 'The Psychoanalytic Psychotherapy of Bulimic Anorexia Nervosa', *Adolescent Psychiatry* 13: 274–314.

—— (1987) 'Panel on Transference and Countertransference in Anorexia Nervosa', paper presented to a Scientific Meeting of the Psychoanalytic Association of New York, 19 November.

—— (1988) 'Bulimic Equivalents', in H. J. Schwartz, ed. (1988b) pp. 489–523.

—— (1992a) 'Ego Functioning and Technique', in Wilson *et al.*, eds (1992), pp. 15–81.

—— (1992b) 'Epilogue', in Wilson *et al.*, eds (1992), pp. 395–413.

—— (1992c) 'Personality Structure and Psychoanalytic Treatment of Obesity', in Wilson *et al.*, eds (1992), pp. 81–99.

——, Hogan, C. C. and Mintz, I. L., eds (1985) *Fear of Being Fat: The Treatment of Anorexia Nervosa and Bulimia.* New York: Jason Aronson.

—— (1992) *Psycho-Dynamic Technique in the Treatment of the Eating Disorders.* New York: Jason Aronson.

Winnicott, D. W. (1941) 'The Observation of Infants in a Set Situation', in *Through Paediatrics to Psycho-Analysis.* London: Hogarth, 1975, pp. 52–70.

—— (1953) 'Transitional Objects and Transitional Phenomena: A Study of the First Not-Me Possession', *International Journal of Psycho-Analysis* 34: 89–97.

—— (1971) *Playing and Reality*. London: Tavistock Publications.

Wooley, S. C. and Wooley, O. W. (1985) 'Intensive Outpatient and Residential Treatment for Bulimia', in D. M. Garner and P. E. Garfinkel, eds (1985), pp. 391–430.

Yarrow, L. J. (1964) 'Parents During Early Childhood', in M. H. Hoffman and I. W. Hoffman, eds, *Review of Child Development Research*, Vol. 1, pp. 89–136. New York: Russell Sage Foundation.

Young, R. M. (1994) *Mental Space*. London: Process Press.

Zeneckis, R. (1993) *Death Becomes Her* (Universal Studios film).

Zerbe, K. J. (1992) 'Eating Disorders in the 1990s: Clinical Challenges and Treatment Implications', *Bulletin of the Menninger Clinic* 56: 167–87.

Zinner, J. and Shapiro, R. (1972) 'Projective Identification as a Mode of Perception and Behaviour in Families of Adolescents', *International Journal of Psycho-Analysis* 53: 523–30.

Index